FINISH
YOUR
DISSERTATION,
DON'T LET IT
FINISH YOU!

Joanne Broder Sumerson

WILEY

Author Photograph: Lisa Kitchen
Cover Design: Wiley
Cover Image: iStockphoto.com

This book is printed on acid-free paper. ⊗

Published by John Wiley & Sons, Inc., Hoboken, New Jersey.
Published simultaneously in Canada.

For general information about our other products and services, please contact our Customer Care Department within the United States at (800) 762-2974, outside the United States at (317) 572-3993 or fax (317) 572-4002.

Wiley publishes in a variety of print and electronic formats and by print-on-demand. Some material included with standard print versions of this book may not be included in e-books or in print-on-demand. If this book refers to media such as a CD or DVD that is not included in the version you purchased, you may download this material at http://booksupport.wiley.com. For more information about Wiley products, visit www.wiley.com.

Library of Congress Cataloging-in-Publication Data:

Sumerson, Joanne Broder.
    Finish your dissertation, don't let it finish you! / Joanne Broder Sumerson, Ph.D.
    1 online resource.
    Includes bibliographical references and index.
    Description based on print version record and CIP data provided by publisher; resource not viewed.
    ISBN 978-1-118-41925-0 (ebk) — ISBN 978-1-118-41635-8 (ebk) —
    ISBN 978-1-118-13303-3 (pbk.)
    1. Dissertations, Academic—Authorship—Handbooks, manuals, etc.   2. Academic writing—Handbooks, manuals, etc.   I. Title.
    LB2369
    808.06'6378—dc23

                                                                    2013020575

Printed in the United States of America

10 9 8 7 6 5 4 3 2 1

This book is dedicated to my loving and supportive husband, Jeffrey. It would still be a bulleted list of ideas on a Post-it note without his daily inquiry, "When are you going to start writing that book already?"

Contents

CONTENTS

Contents

Acknowledgments

Writing this book was a dream come true. Thank you, thank you, thank you to the following people for you being you and for all your support with this book. Words really cannot capture my true appreciation, but I am going to try.

I was very fortunate to work with a talented editorial team, Marquita Flemming, Senior Editor, and Sherry Wasserman, Editorial Program Coordinator, from Wiley. Marquita listened to my ideas and saw their potential for a book, which motivated me to turn this dream into a reality. Her feedback and suggestions were incredibly valuable and improved this book on many levels. I also thank Thomas Caruso, Rose Sullivan, and the rest of the production team who turned this manuscript into a book.

I am blessed to have a network of brilliant colleagues who contributed their wisdom, expertise, and support. Dr. Frank Farley, my former doctoral advisor, Dissertation Chair, and research professor, as well as forever friend and mentor, contributed to this book and taught me the nuts and bolts of solid, strong research practices. Dr. Felice Tilin, my colleague, mentor, dear friend, and big sister shared her consulting model and helped me develop and think through some of these ideas. Dr. Susan Wheelan, my former professor and supervisor, as well as forever mentor and friend, shared her wisdom and allowed me observe those Group and Organizational Research Center meetings, which taught me a great deal about the dissertation process. Dr. James Kaufman, my colleague, co-editor, and newer friend who felt like an old friend the minute I met him, reviewed, advised, and provided guidance that always hit home.

My own dissertation experience was such a positive intellectual and personal journey that I had to write about it, which was partially due to my own committee members from Temple University, Drs. Joseph Ducette, Joseph Rosenfeld, William Fullard, and Trevor Sewell. Thank you to Jack Mayer and Philip Zimbardo, who graciously shared their cherished wisdom with readers. My students at Saint Joseph's University from the Organization Development and Leadership Program give me the honor and privilege to teach and advise them through their thesis and capstone study projects. In addition, I value the content feedback from my colleagues and peers, Dr. Aubrey Wang, Luis Constantino, Joseph Luther, Dr. Goali Saedi, Maritza Santiago, Melissa English Zachowski, and Rose Sutkowski.

The need for Interpersonal Strength is applicable to all goals, and this book was no exception. I am extremely appreciative to have a strong and supportive group of family and friends who are my rock, led by Jeffrey Sumerson, my loving husband, for always making sure I get to write and go to yoga; my sons, Adam and Kyle Sumerson, are my loudest cheerleaders who always keep me on my toes; Michael Broder, my father and colleague, for his love, feedback, review, mentorship, and making me really believe that I can do anything I set my heart on; Sharon Kaufman, my mother,

Acknowledgments

for her unconditional and never-ending love and support that makes my life possible Arlene Goldman, my stepmother and colleague, for her feedback, love, friendship, and perspective; Ken Kaufman, my stepfather, who provides more comic relief than he realizes; and Hesh Weiss, my grandfather and number one fan, for his pride and love, as well as providing me with a peaceful place to write this book while my office was under construction.

In addition, I thank Rachel Zambrano, my unrelated sister, for her sisterhood and a lot of laughs; Pam Jenoff, my best friend for decades and rock-star author, for true friendship and constant inspiration; and Debbie and Harry Nerenberg; Scruft, Carrie, and Lindsay Weiss; Nicole and Adam Malamut; Jennifer Turchin; Toni Noto; Yulla Lamprou Vostaki; Kelly Quinn Sloan; Claire Jones; Sean Browne, Joey Burke; and the late Darryl Norem, as well as Helene and Jim Sumerson, for being there for me more than you know.

Introduction

I was not born an academic, but I somehow morphed into one. I grew up thinking that school was the ultimate torture chamber, a place that specialized in the long, hard, and painfully boring way to learn stuff that did not interest me. I struggled to learn what seemed to come naturally to everyone else. As much as I hated school, I went to college because I had not considered doing anything else. I got through it because I was interested in psychology and needed at least a bachelor's degree to enter the field for the lowest-level positions.

I graduated from college and went straight to jail. My undergraduate college internship at a prison led to a full-time counselor position. It was fun for a while, but I burned out after a few years. Every day, I heard the same story, whether it was from the same or a different inmate, and it got very old. When I tried to strategize my exit from jail, I was hit with the harsh reality that I needed a graduate degree or two or I would be listening to inmates' problems for the rest of my career. I started a master's program at Temple University in Adult and Organization Development (AOD) and left the prison for another job as a corporate human resource generalist. It was in the AOD program where I fell in love with learning. I was so excited to finally feel motivated to learn, as opposed to just getting through course material.

In graduate school, the thought of a dissertation project truly intimidated me—every part of it. There were too many bad ghost stories associated with the dissertation process. Not only did it seem like years' worth of work, but the process seemed to make a lot of people anxious, depressed, and downright miserable. We all heard about (or knew of) people who never finished, had emotional breakdowns, and ended their relationships over their dissertations. According to Glenn (2010) there is a 30% attrition rate in doctoral programs; people start doctoral programs, but do not complete them. Being a part of that 30% was my worst nightmare.

In addition, I did not want to spend multiple years on the dissertation. I had too many goals to achieve, none of which I was eligible for until I earned my doctorate. There were no professional opportunities below a doctoral level that seemed even somewhat interesting, so I felt like I needed to get the hell out of graduate school sooner than later. Time management has always been one of my best survival skills. For better or worse, I have a perpetual habit of spreading myself very thin, so I never have extra time to waste. Thus, a great deal of my practice in this book was developed through the lens of efficiency.

Feeling anxious, depressed, and miserable was also not an option for me. How can the dissertation be an intellectually stimulating project that won't break me? Answering that question was my unofficial research question. Consequently, I did answer that research question through trial and error and figured out what I needed to do to design and deliver a dissertation study—the simple, honest, and productive way — while feeling well balanced and happy. My entire dissertation process from when I broke ground on the proposal to the defense took one calendar year.

On a side note, I also heard horror stories about how so many relationships broke up because of the dissertation. This scared me, too, but the dissertation did not get in the way of my relationship. In fact, it was the opposite for me because my husband, who was incredibly supportive, and I got engaged during my data collection phase, and our wedding date was set for 7 months after my oral defense.

Here I am, many years later, as a professor, research advisor, research psychologist, journal editor, formal Research Review Committee (like an IRB) chair, program evaluator, and, of course, former student, to share the secrets I discovered from successfully navigating my way through the dissertation and thesis process while maintaining sanity and finishing in a timely manner. The purpose of this book is to serve as a friend and unofficial committee member to help you through your dissertation process so that you, too, can join the Doctor's Club and move on with your life to bigger and better things beyond grad school.

The Doctor's Club feels like being a member of a fraternity or sorority. I was a sorority member in college and had several pledging flashbacks during my dissertation process. This experience really helped me understand and appreciate the use of necessary rituals. Instead of proudly wearing a sweatshirt with the Greek letters, you will forever have the letters PhD, PsyD, or EdD after your name and "Doctor" will be your proper salutation.

Most graduate programs in psychology have an extensive list of academic requirements for graduation such as coursework, exams, papers, field work, comps, and, of course, a dissertation or thesis project. Like going through customs when entering another country, you have to successfully go through each checkpoint to gain admittance. Thus, the first thing you have to keep in mind regarding the purpose of this final and important academic requirement is to graduate—get out so you can get in.

I teach graduate-level research and evaluation courses and advise thesis students, both online and in the classroom. Most of my students walk in the door or log on to the first day of the research and evaluation course anxiously dreading their thesis project. My observation is that a lot of the intimidation and angst stems from the lack of realization that they have all the technical skills required to successfully finish their dissertation. We all know the extreme smarty-pants who are still all but dissertation (ABD), so obviously brains are not enough. It's not just being smart—it's learning how to use your brain.

Yoga guru Bikram Choudhury (personal communication, August 24, 2011) described it best when he said, "Having doesn't mean anything if you don't know how to use it."

The PRICE of Your Study

PRICE is an acronym I created for solid and high-quality research: Passion, Rigor, Integrity, Creativity, and Energy to dig deep down to the core essentials of what the dissertation research study needs in order to be a balance between strong and sufficient, so that graduation comes sooner than later. These are the key research rules to remember. Do you have years to devote to your dissertation? I didn't think so! Each of the five PRICE components introduced here will be integrated throughout this book.

Passion

Passion in the context of a dissertation is being in love with the topic so that it feels like your personal mission to create your own research study to learn more about it to satisfy your own curiosity. According to Phillipe, Vallerand, Haulfort, Lavigne, and Donahue (2010), having passion toward something is essential because it could enhance personal identity and motivate one to learn more about the topic. You might not be passionate about doing a dissertation, but the more you love your topic, the more likely you will be Energized and intrinsically motivated enough to design and deliver a Rigorous and Creative study. Having that sense of Passion makes the dissertation process and the small barriers encountered more than bearable, without stressing about the page requirements.

You are probably using your spare time for the dissertation process, so it is crucial that you are Passionate about your topic. Think about it—spending the day in the library on a beautiful summer day can be equally as exciting and gratifying as going to the beach if you love your topic, as opposed to studying a topic that you only semi-love or worse. From my experience, the people who either take a long time to finish or don't finish at all most likely do not have a topic that they genuinely love. There are people out there who are experts in a topic that does not interest them. Do you want to be that person?

Rigor

In the context of research, Rigor ensures that the study is careful, accurate, and the best it can possibly be. High-quality studies are connected to the real world (Schnee, 2008). Glenn (2010) noted that the 30% attrition rate could be due to poor research standards. This is dire, since the purpose of graduate school is to gain preparation for the real world. This book will share what is necessary to maintain high standards for every phase of the dissertation process, from the design and delivery to writing the five main chapters: Introduction, Literature Review, Methodology, Results, and Discussion.

You have to do everything in your power to ensure that the study is Rigorous. Truthfully, it is extra work, but you have to roll up your sleeves and do what you have to do. Choosing credible faculty as committee members will confirm that the study is as Rigorous as possible, since it will make them look bad if your study stinks. Overall, people will not take the study seriously if the study design has too many threats to validity (see Chapter 6), which could disqualify it from getting accepted by your committee, as well as published in a journal or presented at a conference. Of course, every study has limitations, which will be discussed specifically in Chapter 9, but do not use "oh, this will be just another limitation" as an excuse to keep the bar low. If you are Passionate about your topic, you will want to make the study Rigorous to achieve intellectual and intrinsic satisfaction. The study is going to get torn apart anyway, so the more Rigor, the less criticism and fewer revisions—and the more happy committee members!

Integrity

Integrity means complete honesty at every step of the dissertation study process. Behavior should be true and genuine, and the dissertation files, data, and other materials need to be squeaky clean, not just because you could get audited. Integrity is a major theme in this book for each phase of the process.

Dishonesty is a major no-no in general, but especially during the dissertation process. Lack of integrity damages your relationship with stakeholders and places a big, permanent black X over your reputation. Remember, plagiarists, data fudgers, and schnoras (Yiddish for BS artist) get caught!

Creativity

A study designed and delivered with Creativity will be special, unique, and different from the rest. Creativity will ensure that the study contains your personal touch for individual contribution (Kaufman & Beghetto, 2009). Leaders are not leaders because they go with the flow; they are leaders because they determine the flow. Creativity stems from Passion because if you love the topic, the light bulb will keep lighting up with innovative and Rigorous ways to plan and conduct the study, since, according to Kaufman (2009), there are many different ways to be creative.

Without Creativity, the study will not do anything other than recycle other people's research questions. Even if a study is replicated, adopting the methodology from another study and crediting the authors, there are aspects of your study that will vary because it is a different study. Creativity can help you stand out, make your mark, and contribute something valuable to the field. A little creativity goes a long way in a research study, like adding accessories to an outfit.

Energy

Energy is necessary, because it provides the perseverance, motivation, and discipline needed to complete the dissertation. Energy will come from Passion, Rigor, Integrity, and Creativity because you are less likely to get distracted when you combine all of the above. According to Csikszentmihalyi (1991), flow—a natural state of concentration—will occur when there is an intrinsic sense of satisfaction for the activity.

Lack of Energy toward the dissertation topic usually means an incomplete dissertation and ABD. It is difficult to get anything done if there is no Energy. If you are reading this book, you certainly do not want that to be you!

Pre-Study Prep

All projects need physical and psychological space, as well as careful planning, in order to get done. Think about it—to concoct a meal, there needs to be a plan for shopping, preparing, cooking, and serving the food. Kitchen and dining space is the context to store, clean, chop, cook, and eat the food. It is probably easier cooking in a kitchen with which you are familiar. Dissertation and thesis study projects are no exception. Following is a Pre-Study To-Do Checklist that includes a brief explanation of each item.

Pre-Study To-Do Checklist

❑ Realistic work schedule (with extra time built in)

Dissertation and thesis work should be scheduled on the calendar like any other mandatory appointment. You need to be honest with yourself about when you can work on it. Silvia (2010) points out that regularly scheduled time to write needs to be allotted—not found— and writing is a main activity of the dissertation. He emphasizes that the secret to productive writing is a schedule with small goals. Given that most doctoral candidates juggle career and family responsibilities while they work through the dissertation process, strong time management skills are essential. The small goals are generally less daunting and easier to achieve.

Create a work schedule that includes extra cushion time to prevent the embarrassment and frustration of a blown deadline. Life happens, with situations and crises related to careers, families, and ourselves; however, it does not make the dissertation go away. But it is easy to disconnect from it if too much time lapses.

❑ Reliable computer

There are three reasons why I highly advise that you work on your dissertation on a private computer. First, relying on

Introduction

a work or public computer could cause schedule delays in the Realistic Work Schedule, since there is no autonomy for computer access. Second, having a private computer will help convince the IRB (see Chapter 7) that the data will remain completely anonymous and confidential. Third, other people should not be exposed to your dissertation or data until it is ready. Never give anyone the opportunity to delete something important.

Needless to say, if you have your own computer, it will be easier to protect, back up, and lock up. Protect your computer like a parent protects his or her baby!

❑ Space where you work best

Primary and backup working spaces are important factors in finishing the dissertation. A set place to feel comfortable to work can be set up as the primary working space. In the event that the primary space is unavailable, seek out backup work space. Another good reason to find additional space is in case you get bored or feel stuck with the scenery, you have the change you need. There are endless possibilities for backup spaces, including coffee shops, parks, libraries, and friends' homes or offices.

❑ File backup system

Have you ever experienced anything like this nauseating situation? Once upon a time, I worked on my trusty 4-month-old laptop, walked away for a few minutes, and returned to a frozen computer. To make a long and painful story short, I mysteriously lost my hard drive. Thankfully, everything was backed up, so I did not lose files, data, or photos, but I still feel queasy whenever I think about it. Can you imagine losing everything because it was not backed up? Especially since there are so many file backup options. Needless to say, you do not want to be in that situation with your dissertation, so make it a priority to find a backup system that works for you.

There are so many great options out there, and new backup systems are probably being created every day. The cheapest and quickest option is to just e-mail a file to yourself, but having everything backed up on something like a flash drive; online backup system, or an external hard drive is another option. I am a huge fan of the online backup system. It automatically does it for me on a daily basis and does not take up space in my very cluttered office.

❑ Organized place to keep your study materials

Sticky fingers and paws do not mix well with dissertation projects. Keep all dissertation study materials, especially data, in a place that is free of nosy people and fingerprints. You do not want anything lost, damaged, or viewed, so find a place that is out of the way with minimal disruptions. Think of it like the process of doing a large jigsaw puzzle—you would need to do it in a space that is out of the way so the completed sections stay intact and loose pieces do not get lost.

❑ Locked file cabinet

A locked file cabinet is an important piece of equipment to protect data and other sensitive materials from the sticky fingers and paws, as well as nosy people. The IRB (see Chapter 7) also requires that there be a locked file cabinet or storage area in which to keep study materials in order to maintain the Integrity, confidentiality, and anonymity of research participants. Keep all materials related to the study in this cabinet, such as completed surveys, lists, flash drives, and references.

❏ Access to a printer and scanner

Although most of the parts of the dissertation can be e-mailed or uploaded, there might be documents here and there to be printed out. However, reliable access to these is necessary, since there might be a committee member that wants a hard copy of all drafts. Most university computer labs have printers and scanners for student use.

❏ Pre-study certifications

Certifications are the supplemental learning requirements needed to do anything for your dissertation. You can count on the IRB to require a certification that teaches about working with human participants. You must have this certification in order to begin the study. Most university IRBs have a website and an online training certification. Pre-instrument certifications might be necessary, too, such as participation in a training course or completing an application process to use the instrument. Remember to budget time and Energy for certifications into the Realistic Work Schedule.

❏ Interpersonal Strength

There might be only a handful of people who are familiar with the dissertation process and experience, but we could all use Interpersonal Strength and a support system. Know the trustworthy people who care about you. These might be family, friends, colleagues, and fellow ABDs. Reach out to these people when you are feeling tired, burned-out, frustrated, overwhelmed, and in need comfort. These are the folks who will listen to you vent, help you with solutions, and be valuable resources when you are stuck. If these are people outside of the dissertation network, they want to help you but might not know how. It is up to you to ask for the support you need. You know they are only too happy to provide you with emotional or tangible support (child care, coverage at work, helping with errands, and other tasks so you can work on your dissertation) because it might make them feel important during your process.

Do not lean on your committee for emotional support. Chapter 1 explains this in more detail, but their job is to provide technical support, so find other people to whom you can complain and vent.

Priceless Dissertation Wisdom

"Dissertations are often regarded as showcasing an individual's personal scholarship. Increasingly, however, high-quality empirical research is reliant on teams of researchers, because such research requires the integration of expertise at conceptualization, methods, and statistical (or other) models, and few of us can be authorities in all these areas. Doctoral students are team-leaders of sorts: Their team includes any student colleagues they can discuss their research with, as well as members of their dissertation committee. So engage those around you who possess expertise, and let them guide you."

Dr. John (Jack) D. Mayer
Department of Psychology
University of New Hampshire

❑ Know your work style

In the context of a dissertation, your work style is being tuned in to how you work best. Similar to appearance, our personal style determines how we feel our best through choice of clothing, hairstyle, and other accessories. We tend to feel most comfortable and confident when we dress according to our style. For the dissertation study process, owning and embracing your style could help you maximize feelings of Creativity and Energy, which can help make the best use of your work time. For instance, if you like to dress conservatively, how would you feel dressed in Gothic-style clothes? When trying to work under our least favorable conditions, we might not feel our best and do our best work.

To determine your style, go through the Work Style Inventory and check off what best applies to you. Try as hard

Work Style Inventory
(check all that apply to you)

When

- ❏ Morning
- ❏ Afternoon
- ❏ Evening
- ❏ Late night
- ❏ Under pressure
- ❏ Other _____

Where

- ❏ Office (home, work)
- ❏ In transit (on a train, airplane, or bus)
- ❏ Coffee shop
- ❏ Library
- ❏ Anywhere
- ❏ Other _____

How

- ❏ Solitude
- ❏ Complete quiet
- ❏ With people
- ❏ Slight background noise
- ❏ Among hustle and bustle
- ❏ Other _____

Potential Distracters

- ❏ Career
- ❏ Family
- ❏ Procrastination
- ❏ Friends
- ❏ Hobbies
- ❏ Social media
- ❏ Radio and TV
- ❏ Telephone and texts
- ❏ Other _____

as possible to use these preferences to create the ideal environment for you to work on your dissertation and thesis.

These are just a few suggestions and tools to set yourself up for dissertation success. It's time to think about the committee, topic choice, and what is expected in each of the five chapters for the final write-up. Read on!

The Secret Handshake

The dissertation process is a small period of your life for a lifetime membership into the Doctor's Club. It can be challenging on all levels at times, so you need to be smart and strategic as to how you behave and treat people. Interpersonal relationships are such a crucial part of the dissertation process that they are the focus of the first chapter, specifically, dynamics with the Committee and pointers on proper dissertation etiquette. Remember that everyone in the Doctor's Club conquered the same battles as you or they would not be members.

THE TEAM THAT WILL MAKE OR BREAK YOU: THE COMMITTEE

The primary purpose of your dissertation study is to fulfill the final degree requirement and satisfy the Committee; hence, it is not just about you or your study. It is also about the stakeholders interested in this study, such as the Committee. Members of the Committee are your program's professors who mentor, haze, and scare you throughout the dissertation process. Your overall goal is to manage them and keep them happy enough to sign off on your work so you can be done. You need their signatures. *Trust me when I tell you to not even think about fighting or challenging them or the system because you will not win.* If you feel that passionately about an idea they do not like, save it for when you get into the Doctor's Club and shake the secret handshake, but in the meantime, bite your lip and do it their way. Aside from the hazing, Committee Members provide technical support by giving you direction with the study design, theoretical background, research questions, methodology, and data analysis.

The Committee Members invest a great deal of time and Energy by agreeing to work with you, so they obviously think you are worthy enough to be a member of the exclusive Doctor's Club. They might not be all smiles and sunshine toward you, but they are in it for you to win it or they probably would have declined the invitation to serve on your Committee.

Each member should be a balance between a topical content expert and a professor with whom you work well, which, hopefully, you learned through coursework. Ideally, you know him or her well enough to confirm if there is a fit. For instance, if you took a course with a professor and it was a lower than neutral experience, do not put that person anywhere near your dissertation Committee. Save yourself from an unnecessary struggle!

REALITY CHECK

Happy Committee Members sign forms, which turn candidates into graduates.

Typical Dissertation Committee Structure

Most Committees have three members: a Chairperson and two other members. Of course, this varies among universities and programs. The oral defense also includes an examining Chairperson, the person who facilitates the oral defense, and an external Committee Member, which is covered in more detail in Chapter 10. Of course, your Committee will have to approve the external Committee Member. This person can be another faculty member from your department, a colleague, or friend, but he or she is required to have earned a doctorate.

The Chairperson

As the important leader of the dissertation process, the Chair should share your sense of Passion for the topic and seem happy to work with you to design and deliver a great study. If all goes well, ideally, your Chair will collaborate with you on a journal article or conference presentation. Your Chair is typically your doctoral advisor and a professor in your program. It is essential that you have a positive dynamic with your Chair. If he or she is one of those professors who gets on your nerves, don't pick him or her!

As the one in charge of your dissertation process, your Chair should help you pick the other Committee Members, since it is essential they all have a sense of good group dynamics. I highly suggest that you ask your Chair with whom he or she would prefer to work on the Committee. You do not want to pick someone who has bad blood with your Chair. You do not want your study to become ammunition in their battle. The Chair also establishes the structure and protocol for all project phases, such as timing of feedback and when to share drafts with other Committee Members. The Chair is the content, technical, and process expert for the study, but not a part of your interpersonal strength. Remember, you have family members, friends, colleagues, pets, and other ABDs (all but dissertation) for that.

Effective conflict management skills are also very important at this stage. Dramatic conflict with your Chair could easily contribute to getting stuck and possibly not finishing. You do not want your dissertation to be at an impasse because of interpersonal issues.

I feel very fortunate to have worked with the world's greatest dissertation Chair, doctoral advisor, and professor. He was an incredible teacher and always gave valuable advice. Frank is my forever mentor, friend, and colleague, and we continue to work on projects and an executive board together.

General Committee Members

These are two or three additional professors who sit on the Committee, so you should know their interests and, evaluation processes and have a sense of what is it is like to work with them. Students love to tell war stories about professors, so remember to take their experiences with a grain of salt. Quite frankly, most candidates' negative experiences might have stemmed from not navigating the process effectively, such as not following directions or trying to fight the system, which can be an uphill battle. This is similar to the laws of driving, where not respecting the rules of the road and car could cause a traffic ticket, car accident, or damage to the car. Nobody wins in either situation.

In the dissertation process, not following directions will monopolize your time and tarnish your reputation. I knew someone who had trouble with her dissertation Committee because she did not apply their feedback. She did not follow their suggestions because she did not agree with them and was determined to follow her own research agenda. Since she did not listen to them, the Committee refused to sign off on any of her work; thus, she remained at an impasse and would not move forward until she made the changes recommended by the Committee. The bottom line is to just do what they tell you and they will sign the forms so you can graduate.

Do not pick a Committee Member if you can check off any of the following:

- ❏ You know he or she does not like you.
- ❏ You had a negative experience with him or her.
- ❏ You would rate him or her below a neutral on a course evaluation.
- ❏ Your colleagues had a negative experience with him or her that you find to be unacceptable.
- ❏ You get a bad vibe.
- ❏ He or she is known to not get along or work well with your Chair.

"EMILY POST" FOR ACADEMIC RESEARCH

The dissertation and thesis process is one that requires a great deal of lip biting, via emotional intelligence. Salovey and Mayer (1990) described emotional intelligence as being tuned into the emotions of oneself and others to maintain relationships. Candidates who have any negative dynamics with their stakeholders typically do not get their forms signed and their drafts approved. Poor etiquette will only hurt you. Rude people do not get prioritized. Learning to manage yourself and relationships is essential in great leadership (Goleman, Boyatzis, & McKee, 2002). Proper research etiquette is required for all dissertation candidates when interacting with research study stakeholders. Here are my rules for maintaining social and emotional intelligence in the dissertation context.

Top 10 Rules for Maintaining Emotional and Social Intelligence

1. *Know your place.* Although in the outside world you might be the boss, in this context you are an expendable

student, another person and item on everyone's to-do list.

2. *Be humble.* Your Committee is a team of content experts who are all committed to your intellectual development through your dissertation and thesis study. Appreciate their time and avoid any drama. You can show this appreciation by always being prepared and polite. Act like an adult and soon-to-be colleague, never childish.

3. *Kvetch to your* Interpersonal Strength (see Pre-Study To-Do List, pp. xxii–xxviii). Once again, do not even think about complaining to any of the Committee Members—they are not your friends and should not hear your angst. In fact, they might tell you about plenty of people who would appreciate your spot in the program if you are mindless enough to complain to them. They are busy, too, so for every minute you are complaining to them, you are annoying them and occupying time that is better used giving you technical support, which is their role. It's not that we are cold and heartless; we get it and went through it, too. However, we are busy and we are not your therapist. If you vent to the Committee about the process, you are making yourself look bad. Really, what can they do about it? You are not going to get excused from the dissertation and be granted an honorary degree, so save everyone's time and yourself some embarrassment and channel your frustrations elsewhere.

4. *Respect and be very kind to university administrators.* Do not even think about belittling secretaries, project assistants, information technology (IT) folks, and other university staff members, since these are the people who typically rule the roost. If you rub someone the wrong way, you are guaranteed delays because nobody wants to cater to every whim and demand of a pain in the ass. If you have

bad blood with anyone in the university, put this book down and start damage control now.

5. *Eliminate the word* entitled *from your vocabulary*. Doctorates are earned accomplishments, not given to just anyone. You need them and their blessed signatures more than they need you and your attitude. Review Rules 1 and 2.

6. *Stick to the facts when you have obstacles*. If you are going to be delayed, just send an e-mail to your Committee Members to state the facts by telling them when they can expect your next draft.

7. *Think before you speak*. This is the essence of Emotional and Social Intelligence. Use your funnel and say what is appropriate, not what you are thinking and feeling. You cannot take back words and you do not want to put yourself in a bad place or start any drama, heaven forbid.

8. *"Thank you" goes a long way*. Remember, you are appreciative for all the feedback and insight, not disgruntled because it's not what you want to hear or you have more work to do.

9. *Be patient*. Yes, it might be frustrating playing the waiting game, but you have no choice, so deal with it. There are always parts of the dissertation to be completed during downtime.

10. *Make it logistically easy for Committee Members, the IRB, and stakeholders to review drafts*. When resubmitting revised documents, include a memo that lists their suggestions for improvement, the changes you made, and the page number of where they can find the changes in the revised document. This gives the reader a quick and easy way to review the changes without having to search through the document. This saves time for everyone, which is what Covey (1989) would call a win/win situation.

HONESTY REALLY IS THE BEST POLICY

Dishonesty and a lack of Integrity can certainly finish you before you have the opportunity to finish your dissertation. Not only can it get you thrown out of your program and be on your records forever, it will likely make you a high-risk candidate for another program. Dishonesty will damage your brand, so stay on the straight and narrow.

Plagiarism is replicating someone else's work and not giving them the proper acknowledgment for it. It is direct use of someone else's words and claiming them as one's own. Most universities have academic honesty policies that discuss the consequences of plagiarism and other forms of cheating.

I do not look for plagiarized work, but I get "that feeling" when a student's work might be dirty. "That feeling" prompts an investigation, and 30 seconds later, the evidence is confirmed, since the Internet and plagiarism software make it very, very easy to catch plagiarists as well as help you not commit it.

Here is a checklist for keeping on the straight and narrow during the dissertation process.

Checklist for Maintaining Integrity

- ❏ Give credit where credit is due — use citations.
- ❏ Don't change the data, even though they are disappointing.
- ❏ Be as accurate as possible about the time commitment you will need from stakeholders.
- ❏ Be honest about your study's risks and limitations.
- ❏ Do not plagiarize; if you get caught, it's all over.
- ❏ Communicate with your stakeholders and keep them updated about your progress; don't leave them in the dark.
- ❏ Be transparent to participants about study time and activity commitments.

REALITY CHECK

YOU CAN DO IT! When it comes to goal accomplishment, the most important thing is knowing what you need to achieve the goal.

A dissertation is no different than any other big goal. You made it this far, you cannot stop now regardless of your frustration level. You've invested a great deal of time, money, Energy, and emotions into your program, so all you have to do is finish your dissertation, right? If dissertations were easy, everybody would have a doctorate and it would not be that special. Every dissertation encounters barriers that you can and cannot control. You need to learn to work with and around these barriers.

Yes, a dissertation or thesis project can certainly seem overwhelming, big, and never ending. Yes, it is a big project with moments of angst, but do not let it paralyze you. Acknowledge it, let it go, and move on. If this does not work and you truly seem stuck, ask yourself the following:

How Am I Stuck?

- ❑ Do I need to do a better job at managing distractions?
- ❑ Is this the right topic for me?
- ❑ Am I generally tired?
- ❑ Do I need a break from this?
- ❑ Do I need content-oriented help from my Chair or other Committee Members?
- ❑ Do I need to check in with my Interpersonal Strength?
- ❑ Am I burned-out?

Don't be hard on yourself if you do feel stuck. It happens. Look at this list when you are stuck and need some intrapersonal motivation. Here is why you can do it:

- You are indeed smart enough if you made it this far, so it is certainly self-defeating to quit now.
- Your Committee Members really want you to finish and succeed. They accepted you into the program and agreed to work with you on your dissertation Committee because they believe in you.
- You really know what you are doing. Even though you never did a dissertation before, you have probably written five separate papers that have all the elements of the five chapters, which hopefully makes it feel less daunting.
- You will get through these barriers and will have them as future learning experiences.
- You will have this degree forever; you just have to get it.
- Writing and research skills can be developed just like bicep muscles—both can be made stronger with the right conditioning.
- You are only burned-out because you were really on fire!

Prevention strategies for stressful situations include:

- Help writer's block by ending the writing session either mid-sentence or mid-paragraph. It might seem easier to start a new section when you continue from the previous section than to start fresh.
- Find an activity that can help you release stress. After every single meeting with any of my Committee Members, I made it a point to go to the gym. It helped burn off frustration and was a good place to process the meeting before going home.

10

- Meditate, don't obsess—the right idea will come when you least expect it. If you get stuck or bored with a certain section, don't drive yourself crazy and waste your time trying to work on it. Take a break and move on to another section. You can always return to where you left off and will most likely have more ideas to add to it.
- Mind your own business, and do not worry what other people are doing for their dissertations. Their study is their study, and your study is your study—they are different studies with different needs.
- Clear up any bad energy or resolve any looming conflicts with administrators or staff.
- Make sure you take care of yourself during this time with proper nutrition, exercise, and sleep. Take a few days off here and there when you need it to recharge.
- Set small working goals that are achievable and less daunting.
- Remain present and do not obsess about the future. Putting the cart before the horse will only make it more intimidating.
- Find a dissertation buddy—another candidate going through the process—for your Interpersonal Strength so you can support each other.
- Join or form a dissertation support group.
- Connect with your Interpersonal Strength by reaching out to them and asking for what you need.
- Stay connected to your Chair and Committee Members.
- Pace yourself so you do not get burned-out.
- Back up your files every day.
- Do not let too much time pass between work sessions.
- Once again, realize that YOU CAN DO IT!
- Read the list above to get yourself out of a ditch.
- If necessary, start seeing a therapist.

Priceless Dissertation Wisdom

"If you are having trouble getting your thesis on paper, start by writing for just 15 minutes every day. Even if you complete just a few sentences at the end of 15 minutes, it will add up."

Dr. John (Jack) D. Mayer
Department of Psychology
University of New Hampshire

Now that you are emotionally prepared, it is time to get started with your study. You have research to do! The next chapter directs you to the drawing board.

CHAPTER TWO

Breaking Ground on Your Study

The truth about the dissertation that we do not say out loud or put in print is: "The purpose of this dissertation/thesis study is to satisfy the degree requirements and get the hell out of graduate school." The first dissertation chapter, the Introduction, needs a strong "the purpose of this study" statement. It helps to really feel it and have that sense of Passion in order to convince somebody that it is a really important topic.

THE INTRINSICALLY SATISFYING STUDY TOPIC

All dissertation and thesis topics should stem from a topic you love. As mentioned earlier, the Passion is essential. You can turn your Passion into a Rigorous and Creative research study with measurable variables—voilà, the dissertation. As mentioned earlier, you are more likely to achieve Flow (Csikszentmihalyi, 1991), the meditative state of concentration, when you work on your dissertation if you love your topic.

Hopefully, your Chair is Creative and open-minded, so that he or she will facilitate that process with you. It is hard enough to budget the time to do something you are interested in, so doing something where you lack Passion makes it even more difficult. In addition, if the Passion level is low, your Creativity and Energy levels may be low as well. Use Table 2.1 to help flush out ideas into the Intrinsically Satisfying Topic.

In addition to Passion, the topic should have relevance. According to Davis and Parker (1997), a strong dissertation topic should be designed to fill the gaps in current research and practice. If you have a topic in mind and need direction developing it, great sources for ideas can be current events, recommendations for future research from other dissertations and journal articles, and conferences, as well as input from the Committee Members and other scholars.

REALITY CHECK

Note of caution: Do not try to save the world through your dissertation.

Saving the world could make the study bigger and beyond the expectations of your program and Committee. That is a beautiful, altruistic, and amazing concept, but saving the world requires time, money, and extra Energy. Do you really want to invest extra years of your life and money for tuition (that you could put aside to go toward a vacation to celebrate graduation), as well as volunteer to stay on as a student for your dissertation? If your idea is really that exciting, then follow up on it after you earn your degree, when you will have more time, money, and access to resources (e.g., funding, project assistants), and not be paying for credits.

Table 2.1 The Intrinsically Satisfying Topic

	1. Interest Item Keywords	WHAT exactly do I want to know about that Interest Item Keyword?	WHERE exactly do I want to learn more about these constructs?	WHOM do I want to study?	CONFIRM: Why do I want to study this?
Meditate on this:					
Ask yourself:	What buzz-words really, really interest me?	What will really satisfy my curiosity about these buzzwords?	Which particular context or setting interests me?	What type of person interests me?	How will studying this topic help me to advance my professional and personal development? How will this topic help other people?
My dissertation topic as an example:	Personality types, Motivation, and Preferred Learning Strategies	To learn more about the intrapersonal factors that impact how students achieve content mastery	College and university setting	Undergraduate and graduate level students	**Topic: Examination of the relationship between personality, motivation, and preferred learning strategies to predict academic achievement (grade point average)**

(Continued)

15

Table 2.1 The Intrinsically Satisfying Topic (Continued)

One of my dream studies:	Team dynamics, winning athletic (football) teams	To learn more about the relationship between group process (stage of group development) and NFL team performance	Professional football team performance (as measured by team record)	Teams representing the National Football League	**Topic: An Examination in the Relationship Between NFL Team Performance and Group Process (as measured by the Group Development Questionnaire,** Wheelan & Hochberger, 1996)
					As a researcher, professor, and consultant of group process as well as football fan, the data would be very interesting to me.

In retrospect, I chose this topic as a budding college professor and my study has since helped me understand my students so I can successfully facilitate their learning process.

Passion and Rigor are also essential ingredients in the dissertation study, but you have to keep boundaries around them so that you can stick to the Realistic Work Schedule and finish in a timely manner. Take the project for what it is: It is a large and intense research study that needs to be completed with the level of quality that meets the expectations of the university and your program. The dissertation study should be exciting to you, but simple and measurable to prevent your being an all but dissertation (ABD) forever. Read on—this book will coach you on not making that mistake.

Priceless Dissertation Wisdom
"Don't linger, complete the dissertation, and get out. Your life awaits."

Dr. Frank H. Farley
Temple University
Former APA President

BREAKING GROUND CAN BE EASIER THAN YOU THINK

Similar to painting that first splash of color to a blank canvas, opening a new document or blank page and writing that first word can be very intimidating. Every single project has to start somewhere, but it does not have to be stressful. For instance, this book is an example that all big projects begin with at least one bullet point. To start brainstorming, you need a trusty note-taking system. Jae Ho Park (2013) promotes the Idea Racing System, which is journaling through unstructured writing, pictures, notes, and ideas as a base. The most important thing is to record those ideas so that they are not lost. Once the ideas are down, even the most informal notes, you have officially gotten started. Think about snowballing, because all you have to do is develop those ideas by building more ideas on top of them.

I am a fan of taking notes and jotting down ideas in a journal-style notebook. However, I am also known to dictate notes into my phone, later to be transferred into my notebook. I prefer the old-fashioned handwritten process for taking notes, but everybody does what works for them. There are even apps for our phones that help us with note taking and plotting out various mind map charts.

THE QUICK AND DIRTY ABOUT VARIABLES

Variables are the buzzwords that provide the general shape and structure for the study. In the context of psychological research, these keywords or constructs are the observable traits and states consistent with behavioral patterns. The entire study stems from the variables, which are turned into measurable constructs. Most constructs are measurable to a degree (Reynolds, 2010), but you and the Committee need to be Creative and make the study as Rigorous as possible. Similar to constructing a building, the first step is to decide the type of structure and its purpose. Is this building going to be a house, school, hospital, or office building?

Let's say we decided to build a house; we have now defined the building. We know the house should be built with all the features of a house and neither a school nor hospital.

As seen in Figure 2.1, this is a single ranch-style house with one floor as well as a basement and attic. The view shows the interior and exterior to get a visual of what a ranch-style house looks like. Each of these are discussed in more detail later in this book.

Figure 2.1 The Similarities Between a House (Internal and External View) and a Research Study
Source: Kevin Moss.

Similarities Between the Elements of a House and Research

- Building type: Residential one-family house (variables).
- House essentials: Structure, Foundation, and Frame (research questions).
- House style: Ranch style, one floor including a basement and an attic (research design).
- House flow and features: The look and physical characteristics of the house (literature review).

Dependent Variables

Dependent variables are the outcome, result, or end product under investigation. We look at the dependent variables under the influence of independent variables. At the end of the day, dependent variables tell us results such as quantity, intensity, quality, and duration. Examples of dependent variables include sales dollars, retention rates, productivity level, satisfaction level, depression level, and other outcome data from assessments that measure knowledge, individual traits, attitudes, or aptitude.

Independent Variables

Independent variables are different groups examined for the degree to which they do or do not influence the dependent variables. The groups are based on specific types of characteristics (people who are in one group or another group, such as men and women or people who are employed and unemployed), conditions (experimental and control group), and construct groups (depressed and nondepressed people). Their purpose is to see how the variety between or within the groups impacts the outcome. For example, if we examined the relationship between personality type and grade point average, the independent variable would be personality type (e.g., introvert and extrovert), and grade point average, which is already calculated by the college or university, would be the dependent variable.

Levels Within the Variables

Each variable will most likely have to be broken into subgroups, which are levels, domains, categories, dimensions, and lots of other names, depending on the program. The number of levels will change per variable. It will depend on the type of variable as well as how you decide to study it. For instance, gender is a variable with two levels (male and female), which is also known as a dichotomous variable. However, age group can be a dichotomous variable (adults between 18 and 44 or 45 and above) or a seven-level variable (adults from 18 to 30, 31 to 40, 41 to 50, 51 to 60, 61 to 70, 71 to 80, and 81+), depending on what you really want to know. In general, you can divide your variables into whatever types of levels work for you. Another example of a multilevel independent variable would be one with three levels, like participants' community setting, such as urban, suburban, and rural.

VARIABLE DEFINITIONS

Each variable needs to be clearly defined so that the reader knows exactly what the constructs mean. Variables can be defined two different ways: conceptually and operationally (Pyrczak & Bruce, 2000). Conceptual definitions are the variable's theoretical terms from cited references. The literature review will include conceptual definitions of the variables, since empirically based frameworks are discussed. Operational definitions are the concrete and physical definition of the variable specific to meet the needs of your study. This is your definition and is mentioned in the Methodology chapter.

If the use of chocolate were an independent variable, the lit review would include the conceptual definition of chocolate through the discussion of research, background, theories, historical trends, and other published relevant information that connect to the variable. The operational definition would tell the reader the type, quantity, and dosage of chocolate used in the study, (e.g., four Hershey's Hugs per participant, which were half milk and half white chocolate). Another example could be the extrovert personality trait. The conceptual definition would be the theoretical description from personality theories and studies. The operational definition would determine whether someone is an extrovert because of a score within a validated range.

THIS IS EXACTLY WHAT I WANT TO KNOW: ASK SOLID RESEARCH QUESTIONS

Once the variables are confirmed, it is time to break them down and write one research question for each variable under investigation. The purpose of any research study is to answer the research questions so they must be clear, concise, measurable, and 100% blessed by the Committee.

The research questions need to be on the radar at all times, since they drive the entire study. The literature review and methodology are directly linked to the research questions. The literature review includes the theoretical models and empirical data that either support or challenge the variables and how they will be measured. The methodology is created with the leading question: "What is the best way to answer these research questions?"

The research questions serve as the study's solid and sturdy foundation. Similar to a house with a weak foundation, the research questions need to be strong or the study will collapse. Going back to our house example on pages 18 to 19, you would also not want to build a school on top of a base shaped for a house, so every part of the study needs to be directly linked to the research questions.

The five chapters tell the long and drawn-out story about the study. Research questions and hypotheses typically do not appear until the Methodology chapter; therefore, create the research questions first and design the study around answering those questions. The research questions need to be worded clearly and precisely or quality of the study and final write-up will not be clear.

Strong, solid, and precise research questions are:

- Written concisely with as few words as possible.
- Clear so that the readers know what the data attempt to answer.
- Open-ended and rich, beginning with *what* or *how* and written so that they lead to unguided responses, even with quantitative data. Closed-ended questions that start with *do* or *is* can be answered by yes/no, are limited, and lack rigor. For example, a question like *How does amount of time spent per day on Facebook influence divorce rates?* is a richer question than *Does the amount of time per day spent of Facebook relate to divorce rates?* They ask the same thing, but to answer the first question, you need a holistic response as opposed to the second question, which can give you a simple answer like a yes/no type of response. Save those simple questions for the data collection instrument items, whose purpose is to get the data that ideally answer the research questions.
- Nonbiased and nondirectional, save your opinion for the hypothesis.
- Contains words such as *influence, contribute, impact, relate,* and *compare.*
- Avoid words such as *cause, effect,* or any other presumptuous words (this is one of the understood rules in psychology). People are not predictable like machines.
- Created for each variable. However, you do not have to provide a research question for the variable's individual levels. For example, if gender was the independent variable, the research question would include gender as

opposed to writing separate research questions for males and females.

- Directly linked to the statistic used for the data analysis in order to answer the research question. Include only the dependent and independent variables that need to be examined together per question. For instance, if you looking at relationships and are doing a simple Pearson r, include only the two variables you are looking to analyze. Throw more than two variables into the question and it will need a multiple regression analysis. Write simple questions if you plan to use simple statistics; the more complex the question the harder the statistic.
- 100% blessed by each Committee Member.

Following are examples of strong research question stems as well as bad and good research questions. Remember, when more variables are added, a higher level statistic will need to be applied for the analyses. These questions will be simple for the sake of the example.

Examples of Strong Research Question Stems

- How does _____ influence _____?
- What is the relationship between _____ and _____?
- How does _____ compare to _____ in _____?
- What are the trends in _____ since _____?

Examples of Bad Research Questions

- How does Facebook impact relationships?
- Which alcohol treatment group (full intervention, partial intervention, no intervention) is the best?

- Do pets help with depression?
- What happens when you mix personality, motivation, learning strategies, and the SAT with grades?
- Do Millennials post more often on Facebook and Twitter than Baby Boomers?

Examples of Good Research Questions

- How does number of Facebook postings per day impact relationship fidelity rate?
- How do the alcohol treatment groups (full intervention, partial intervention, no intervention) compare in their sobriety rates?
- What is the relationship between pet ownership (pet owners and non–pet owners) and depression levels?
- How do personality traits, motivation levels, the use of learning strategies, and SAT score relate to academic achievement as measured by GPA?
- How do generation groups compare in the number of Facebook and Twitter posts per day?

REALITY CHECK

Trying to understand a study with poorly written research questions is like trying to understand a person talking with food in his or her mouth—they both sound mumbled.

Good research questions clearly and specifically tell us what we want to know. They will keep us focused as we conduct our study, research, and write the five chapters.

This Is What I Think About What I Want to Know: Confident Hypotheses

According to Creswell (2009), the research question inquires about the relationship among the variables and needs a corresponding hypothesis, which predicts what is going to happen within the variables. A hypotheses is the educated guess of what the answer might be to the research question. *Your research questions and hypotheses should mirror each other*. You should check in with your program requirements to determine whether you have to write a null hypothesis, a separate hypothesis that states the opposite result of your hypothesis among the variables. If not, then state your general hypothesis in a clear, strong, and confident response to these two questions:

- What do you think the answer will be to that research question?
- Why do you think that?

Including the "why" strengthens the hypothesis. Even one additional sentence goes a long way.

Reality Check

Picture yourself rolling dice. Which numbers will the dice show? Why do you predict those numbers?

The data you collect for the study should either support or challenge the hypothesis. If the study results contradict your hypotheses, so be it. Learn from it and move on. Hypotheses proven to be wrong (or accepting the null hypothesis) will not stop you from graduating. Do not compromise integrity

by tweaking the data in order to support your hypotheses. The truth may come out anyway, and with unwanted consequences.

Be prepared to support the hypotheses through theory and practice. There needs to be a strong rationale for them, especially if Committee Members and other stakeholders challenge your hypotheses (which is to be expected), so be armed and ready for your intellectual argument, with theory and research as the weapons.

Following are examples of research questions with their corresponding hypotheses. I personally like it written up this way in the Methodology chapter.

Examples of Research Questions and Hypotheses

RQ 1: How does the number of Facebook postings per day impact relationship fidelity rates?

    HY 1: The number of Facebook postings per day will show an impact on relationship fidelity. The higher the number of Facebook postings, the lower the fidelity rates because people are spending more time with social media than working on their relationships.

RQ 2: How do the alcohol treatment groups (full intervention, partial intervention, no intervention) compare in their sobriety rates?

    HY 2: The full-intervention treatment group will have higher sobriety rates than the partial or no intervention groups. The more exposure participants will have with the affective, behavioral, and cognitive skills associated with sobriety, the more likely they are to stay sober.

RQ 3: What is the relationship between pet ownership (pet owners and non–pet owners) and depression levels?

    HY 3: People who own pets will reveal lower levels of depression than people who do not own pets. Animals show people love and give them a sense of daily purpose to care for them, which could help people feel happier and less depressed.

Priceless Dissertation Wisdom

"Find a topic that you really care about and want to learn more about. Read journal articles and books on your topic. Read your brains out. Determine what your research question will be. Then follow the directions of your advisor."

Susan A. Wheelan, PhD, President
GDQ Associates, Inc.
Mother of Group Dynamics

After you think through what you want to do, you should have a clear idea of what is expected of you. The next chapter provides a blueprint that explains the contents of each chapter so you can start meditating (and not obsessing) on how you are going to carry through your dissertation study.

CHAPTER THREE

Anatomy of a Dissertation

The five chapters tell the full story about your study. In a nutshell, they include why it is important (Introduction), theoretical perspective and prior empirical evidence (Literature Review), data collection process (Methodology), data analyses (Results), and data interpretation (Discussion). There is a chapter in this book for each chapter of the dissertation write-up.

This is the typical layout of the first five chapters of the final dissertation write-up. The Anatomy of a Dissertation in Table 3.1 lists each chapter's subsections and important points and was based on an analysis of 35 websites from social science programs located in the United States. The samples were programs from colleges and universities that diversified in terms of size (small, medium, and large), religious affiliation (or not), funding type (private or public), level of prestige and competiveness (Ivy League and non–Ivy League), and amount of research focus. The layout of the dissertation and thesis might slightly vary per program, so definitely confirm your individual program's requirements.

Table 3.1 Anatomy of a Dissertation

	Introduction Chapter (Chapter 1)	
Chapter Subsection	**Includes**	**Points to Remember**
Introduction	• Cited literature to set the stage for your study. • Trends, issues, background of this topic.	• Grab reader's attention with first sentence.
Rationale	• Statements regarding importance of topic. • Detailed explanation of the problem. • Mention of gaps in the literature or lack of knowledge in practice.	• Continue to convince the reader with why a study on this topic was needed.
Purpose of Study	• A clear statement that stems from "the purpose of this study was to . . ." • Expansion of this to talk about how your data could be applied to improve a situation.	• Purpose statement should be strong, crisp, and pithy. • Include a brief description of the methodology. • Discuss the relevance of data and how it will be used to improve this and that.

Literature Review Chapter (Chapter 2)

Chapter Subsection	Includes	Points to Remember
Review of Literature	• Synthesis of published, peer reviewed, and scholarly work of theory, models, empirical data, and case studies for each variable. • Sets the frame of your perspective. • Point out historical trends, themes, and gaps.	• This chapter is typically organized by variable. • If you were not the very first one to say, research, or notice it, then it must be cited. • More is always better when it comes to empirical evidence from previous research studies. • Use citations over quotations. • Use direct quotes only to make a strong statement. • Expect many, many drafts.
Conceptual Definitions	• Description of each dependent and independent variable, as explained in the literature.	• This is different from the operational definition that belongs in the Methodology chapter.

(Continued)

Table 3.1 Anatomy of a Dissertation   (*Continued*)

	Methodology Chapter (Chapter 3)	
Chapter Subsection	**Includes**	**Points to Remember**
Research Questions and Hypotheses	• One hypothesis per research question.	• The research questions are the foundation for the entire study. • They should echo each other. • Format so that they look like this: RQ 1: HY 1: RQ 2: HY 2:
Research Design	• Description of research design and how it was chosen for the study. • How the data will be analyzed.	• The type of study, number of groups involved. • The brief overview of the data analysis more big picture information, as opposed to detail.
Operational Definitions	• Brief definition of independent and dependent variables.	• This definition is concrete and measurable (e.g., how much, how often, those who scored between x and y on an instrument). • Differs from the conceptual definition in the literature review, in that it is not theoretical.

Participants	• Description of participants. • What made them eligible for the study. • How they were recruited for your study. • Description of any compensation.	• Provide a very clear picture of study sample. • Mention how you maintained their privacy.
Instruments and Materials	• Detailed description of any surveys, activities, programs, and other materials used for your study. • Rationale for using those materials. • For published instruments, should include a summary of the validation process and other psychometric properties to support its robustness. • For homemade surveys, talk about the validation process to support that it will basically be "good enough" or the only option for your study.	• Provide a clear visual for the reader about the looks of your materials and their length of administration. • Surveys and other study materials belong in the appendices. • Be confident in your explanation as to why the instrument and materials were used.
Procedure	• Detailed description of what you did when you collected the data. • Tell the reader the story from start to finish.	• The more detail, the better so that anyone could replicate your procedure to the letter.

(Continued)

33

Table 3.1 Anatomy of a Dissertation   (Continued)

	Results Chapter (Chapter 4)	
Chapter Subsection	**Includes**	**Points to Remember**
Introduction	• Brief summary of the purpose of the study and method. • Description of the process or application for data analysis.	• Short, sweet, and to the point. • Just say what you did to analyze it.
Descriptive Data	• Frequency analyses of number and percentage of relevant demographic groups (e.g., gender, age group, nationality, etc.).	• You do not have to include any SPSS codes. • You may have a table for this.
Analysis of Research Questions and Hypotheses	• Each research question and hypothesis with a table or figure of the data that either supports or challenges the hypothesis. • Brief mention whether it supports or challenges the research cited in the literature review.	• Write statistics in proper format (see statistical chart in Appendix A). • Eliminate bias; the data should be unfolded and connected very objectively. • Tell it like it is. • Don't skimp on the real evidence.
Additional Analyses	• Other observations or patterns in your data that you find are worth mentioning. • Brief mention on how it fits into the literature.	• Write statistics in proper format (see statistical chart in Appendix A). • Eliminate bias; the data should be unfolded and connected very objectively. • Tell it like it is. • Don't skimp on the real evidence.

Discussion Chapter (Chapter 5)

Chapter Subsection	Includes	Points to Remember
Introduction	• Very brief summary of the purpose of the study, method, and how the data were analyzed.	• Short, sweet, and to the point.
Interpretation of Findings	• Organize per research question. • Talk about the results, their meaning, their connection to the literature, and how the data could be used.	• Be creative; this is one of the fun parts.
Limitations	• Any limitations noted about the study.	• Swallow your pride and be humble; every study has them.
Implications for Theory and Practice	• Your interpretation of the overall meaning of the data, as well as how it fits into the literature and "real world."	• Be assertive. • Think of this as settling the argument in the literature. • You are the expert!
Next Steps and Recommendations for Future Research	• How you can possibly expand your study • In hindsight, what else needs to be studied in that topic area.	• Have fun and be creative.
clusion	• Ties it all together	• Short, sweet, and to the point.

What Comes Before the Five Chapters

The dissertation and thesis does not start with the Introduction. The following elements precede the first chapter and should be formatted as per the guidelines in the *Publication Manual of the American Psychological Association* (6th ed.; American Psychological Association [APA], 2010). See Appendix B for Anatomy of a Dissertation in Context, which shows you what goes into each chapter, with some formatting guidance.

- *Title page*. The title page includes your name, dissertation or thesis title, institution, running head, and the words "In partial fulfillment for the degree requirement _____." Insert your degree there.
- *Abstract*. The abstract should be a pithy summary of the study that includes the problem, purpose, brief description of method, general conclusions, and implications. For the proposal, the abstract should be written in future tense; use past tense with a quick summary of the results for the final write-up.
- *Table of contents*. The table of contents tells the reader where to find each chapter, subchapter, table, figure, and appendix.
- *Dedication*. A dedication is not necessary, but it is a very nice thing to do.
- *Acknowledgments*. The acknowledgments section gives you the opportunity to thank the Committee, Interpersonal Strength, and Network for their friendship, love, encouragement, support, and guidance. I personally think it is tacky when people do not have an acknowledgment. Never forget where you came from or the people who supported you while you achieved success.

WHAT FOLLOWS THE FIVE CHAPTERS

By the time you finish the discussion, you are likely to be feeling "done"; however, you are not "done." But there are only two more subsections until it is officially finished. They are the references and appendixes.

- *References.* This section must be formatted APA style (see *Publication Manual of the American Psychological Association*; APA, 2010). Every single reference needs to be listed in this section.
- *Appendixes.* Each separate document in the appendixes should be named and numbered. These documents are usually important parts of the dissertation that might be too big to place in the body of the text, including but not limited to instruments, participant recruitment protocols, raw data, tables, figures, and pictures. It depends on your Committee's requirements.

ADDITIONAL HELPFUL RESOURCES

Anatomy of a Dissertation in Context: see Appendix B.

Cooper, H. (2011). *Reporting research in psychology: How to meet journal article reporting standards.* Washington, DC: American Psychological Association.

Cone, J., & Foster, S. (2006). *Dissertations and theses from start to finish: Psychology and related fields* (2nd ed.). Washington, DC: American Psychological Association.

Duhigg, C. (2012). *The power of habit: Why we do what we do in life and business.* New York, NY: Random House.

Pryrczak, F., & Bruce, R. B. (2000). *Writing empirical research reports* (3rd ed.). Los Angeles, CA: Pryrczak.

Sample Rubric to Evaluate Dissertations: see Appendix C.

CHAPTER FOUR

Rolling Out the Red Carpet for Your Study: The Strong Introduction

The first chapter of the dissertation, Introduction, needs to powerfully grab the reader's attention. It is the shortest of the five chapters and meant to convince the readers that this study is important and the data will benefit its intended population and system. The three subsections, the Introduction, Rationale, and Purpose of Study are similar to what Silberman (1998) called "What, So What, Now What?"

Table 4.1 outlines the contents of the Introduction, broken down by the three subsections and what they should contain.

Table 4.1 Introduction At-a-Glance From Anatomy
of a Dissertation

Introduction Chapter (Chapter 1)		
Chapter Subsection	Includes	Points to Remember
Introduction	• Cited literature to set the stage for your study. • Trends, issues, background of this topic.	• Grab reader's attention with first sentence.
Rationale	• Statements regarding importance of topic. • Detailed explanation of the problem. • Mention of gaps in the literature or lack of knowledge in practice.	• Continue to convince the reader why a study on this topic was needed.
Purpose of Study	• A clear statement that stems from "the purpose of this study was to . . ." • Expansion of this to talk about how your data could be applied to improve a situation.	• Purpose statement should be strong, crisp, and pithy. • Include a brief description of the methodology. • Discuss the relevance of data and how it will be used to improve this and that.

INTRODUCTION (*WHAT* IS GOING ON HERE?)

Every study needs a strong introduction to capture and hold the reader's attention (Creswell, 2009). A strong introduction reads more like a Problem Statement since it includes data, theoretical models, current issues, and overall trends on the variables. For instance, if you were doing a study on Internet addiction, you would want to start off with some alarming statistics and trends about it, as cited by references, such as "X number of people suffer from Internet addiction." This tells the reader, wow, this topic is important. First, assert the issue, then the Rationale, which establishes the issue, before you declare the Purpose of the Study.

RATIONALE (*SO WHAT* MAKES THIS TOPIC IMPORTANT?)

Now that the study has been introduced and the reader's attention is piqued, the Rationale discusses the importance of these variables and the lack of necessary information by highlighting the gaps in the research, literature, knowledge base, and practice. The argument built in this subsection makes an excellent predecessor to the purpose of your particular study, which will ideally help fill those gaps.

PURPOSE OF STUDY (*NOW WHAT* IS GOING TO BE DONE ABOUT IT?)

The stage set should be so compelling that naturally, the next section will tell the reader how data from this study will fill a gap with strong and pithy words to explain, *the purpose of this study is to* _____. This section also briefly mentions the methodology and emphasizes how the data will be used to improve a theory, system, practice, or population. It has to be relevant and linked to the issues discussed in the previous two sections.

Proposal Versus Final Write-Up

The difference between the Introduction chapter in the proposal and the final write-up is the tenses. The proposal uses future tense, since you have not conducted the study yet; and the final write-up is in past tense because the study was already done.

CHAPTER KILLERS

Introduction Chapter Killers

You are begging Committee Members for revisions if you do any of the following:

- Use of first person—dissertations and theses should be written in the third person.
- Leave out cited references and data.
- Include other parts of the study that do not belong in the Introduction.
- Write purpose statements that are wordy, confusing, or weak.
- Not change the verb tenses from the proposal to the final write-up.
- Discuss data that are neither linked nor connected to the study variables.

Purpose of Study (*Now What* Is Going to Be Done About It?)

Now that you've made a compelling argument as to why your study should be done and its benefits in the larger world, you need to think about the theoretical perspectives for your variables. The Introduction rolls out the red carpet for the study that leads you to the stage. The Literature Review sets the stage for the study by presenting the theoretical background, empirical evidence, and conceptual definitions of the variables.

CHAPTER FIVE

Literature Review Made Simple

A literature review is the theoretical explanation and empirical evidence to support and challenge the variables. Theoretical models published in journal articles and books attempt to validate the variables (Thorndike, 1982). Ideally, these models are based on empirical evidence. The literature review needs to be directly linked to your variables and research questions, which will keep it streamlined throughout the research and writing phases. It needs to be a balance between focused and detailed. You do not want to ramble or go off on tangents. Keep the research questions close by and think about how each source helps share insight about them. Going back to our house example in Chapter 2, the theoretical perspective gives the house its unique sense of style, flow, and features, such as the fireplace and location of the stairs (Figure 2.1). These features give the house a sense of character, organization, and direction. It sets the stage for your study. For instance, if your study involved a personality measure, are you going to use the NEO Five Factor Inventory to measure the Big Five (Costa & McRae, 1995) or another personality model?

The length will vary by program requirements, but count on its being very, very long, at least 50 to 75 pages. It might feel like you are going on and on forever because, quite frankly, you do. However, this needs to be done without babbling. Table 5.1 shows the elements of the Literature Review.

HOW TO DO AN EXEMPLARY LIT REVIEW

Most psychological constructs have preexisting theoretical models and data published in scholarly books and peer-reviewed journals. Your Literature Review will be many, many pages explaining the study variables, and connecting them to global issues on the topic via published literature. The literature review gives the study direction, as well as builds up the argument as to why this topic and these variables are important. In our house in Chapter 2, it gives it flow and unique features.

Since the purpose of the study is to thoroughly answer the research questions, it is time to look for scholarly empirical and theoretical evidence to support or challenge the study's rationale, hypotheses, design, results, and implications.

The literature review aligns your study with what is being done and/or what has been done in your field. Overall, an exemplary literature review calls for:

- References from peer-reviewed journals and published books. The more, the merrier, but make sure you evaluate them for high quality (see the Juicers later in this chapter).
- Conceptual definitions of variables described through theoretical models, frameworks, and other paradigms.

Table 5.1 Literature Review At-a-Glance From *Anatomy of a Dissertation*

Literature Review Chapter (Chapter 2)

Chapter Subsection	Includes	Points to Remember
Review of Literature	• Synthesis of published, peer reviewed, and scholarly work of theory, models, empirical data, and case studies for each variable. • Sets the frame of your perspective. • Points out historical trends, themes, and gaps.	• This chapter is typically organized by variable; many, many drafts will help you determine the right sequence for your study. • If you were not the very first one to say, research, or notice it, then it must be cited. • More is always better when it comes to empirical evidence from previous research studies. • Use citations over quotations. • Use direct quotes only to make a strong statement. • Expect many, many drafts.
Conceptual Definitions	• Description of each dependent and independent variable, as explained in the literature.	• This is different from the operational definition that belongs in the Methodology chapter.

- Empirical evidence from high-quality research studies.
- Historical trends and themes in the literature.
- Gaps, issues, and other concepts explored for each of the variables.
- Conflicting research and perspectives for the variables — maybe your study will resolve the issue.
- Sources that are current and up to date.
- Other statistics on the number of people impacted by the variable.
- Organization by variable, methodology, or some other way so that it flows.
- Paraphrased references appropriately summarized and cited. Paraphrasing is writing the gist of the source content, sharing the overall big picture.
- Sources synthesized together, discussed as they support and challenge each other, as opposed to an annotated bibliography, which discusses each source separately.
- Use of direct quotes only to make a point, when you really cannot paraphrase it.
- Well written and free of grammatical issues — remember, good writing skills can always be developed. The good news is that you will do so much writing, it is bound to improve throughout the dissertation process!

GIVE THE AUTHOR PROPER CREDIT

This book promotes 100% Integrity, which needs to be clearly reflected when appropriately citing the work of other authors. Refer to the sixth edition of the APA *Publication Manual* (APA, 2010) for the proper way to cite every type of source, from scholarly books to journal articles, websites, and personal communication. Remember, plagiarists practically always get caught.

As mentioned, I catch plagiarists when my gut tells me something is not right and I have to start checking sources. Most of the time when I check, I do find evidence of plagiarism, by finding that their work was copied and pasted directly from another person's work, which is cheating and could result in getting kicked out of the program or university for good.

Your opinion and experiences do not belong in a literature review unless you are citing your own work, since it is entirely a collection of past work done on the topic. The only information you need in the citation is the author's last name and the year of the source. The page number is added for direct quotes.

JUICE YOUR SOURCES FOR THE INFORMATION YOU NEED

The amount of scholarly reading required for a dissertation can be daunting and confusing. The Literature Review needs many different sources and some may be more useful than others. It is very important to stay focused and extract the information that is right for your Literature Review, not just because it is there. Similar to juicing an orange, you want to squeeze out what you want and leave out what you do not need. The fact that something is published does not mean the data are from a good study and a well-written article; it might simply mean that the authors got lucky with a panel of easy reviewers. Thus, it is essential that you consider the results with a critical eye.

There is no research study that is perfect, and anyone who tries to convince you otherwise probably sells bridges to grad students on the side. Most have some sort of threat to Internal and External Validity. Or their data are based on a study with threats to Internal and External Validity, even if they are small. There are lots of studies that support and challenge those studies, too.

Threats to Internal and External Validity

These study limitations influence the data. Campbell and Stanley (1963), in their seminal work on behavioral research, describe threats to Internal and External Validity that could impact study results. These threats are timeless in that they are comparable to current descriptions.

Internal Validity

- Use of invalid instruments and other weak data collection items.
- Biases in participant sample.
- Historical events that might have impacted the data.
- Study conditions that might cause people to act differently from their version of normal.

External Validity

- Generalizing the study results of a homogeneous sample (e.g., undergraduate college students enrolled in an Introduction to Psychology course) to the global population.
- Data results or behaviors not correlating with similar measures of the same construct.

Below are Juicers that will help you extract the key information you need from each source. There are two types of Juicers: Empirical and Theoretical. They are described in more detail later, but their main difference is that Empirical (or experimental) sources collect and report original data, and Theoretically based sources do not but instead report on other study results. The purpose of juicing is that you have the relevant information you need from each reference. This should prevent you from having to print out or photocopy articles and book chapters. Juice out what you need for when you start writing; all of your references will be summarized and organized, and you will have a clear idea as to how they fit into the proposal and final dissertation write-ups. I find it to be more efficient to write from a stack of summaries than from a bunch of articles and books scattered around me. Here are the steps for using Empirical and Theoretical Juicers.

How to Use the Juicers

1. Make several copies of each blank Juicer found in Appendix D.
2. Use one per source to summarize what you need to know, guided by your research questions.
3. Answer the questions under each Juicer item to extract relevant information for the literature review.
4. Organize sources by chapters and variables. Some sources may be used in multiple chapters, so have a way to distinguish them from the rest. You do not want to miss anything good!
5. Synthesize.
6. Write.

Empirical Juicer

Experimental study data and processes need to be evaluated with a critical eye in order to determine if it is worth mentioning in the lit review. This form should help you juice key information that you particularly need and evaluate the quality of an experimental study with a keen eye so you understand the perspective of the published study results. Following is each component of the form, with guiding questions to help you focus on what you need from that source. These components are explained in more detail in Chapter 6, which discusses all the components of the Methodology. Not all articles clearly mention this information, but get what is relevant to help theoretically address your research questions and pull out enough detail from the article to talk about it.

Full reference: According to the sixth edition of the *Publication Manual of the American Psychological Association* (APA, 2010).

Purpose of study: What did they try to do?

Argument/Logic developed in the literature review: What was their theoretical perspective?

Research questions: What did they really want to know?

Hypothesis: What was their educated guess?

Research design: What was the type of study?

Participants: What were the characteristics of the people who participated in the study?

Independent variables: What were the variables that influenced the outcomes?

Dependent variables: What were the study outcome variables?

Instrumentation/Materials: What did they use to collect data — surveys, interview protocols, trial and training materials, as well as programs, software, and technology?

Procedure:

How did they collect data?

What did they do with the participants?

How did they analyze their data?

What were the statistical analyses?

General conclusions: What were the study's outcomes?

Implications: What do the results mean?

Study strengths: What did they do really well?

Limitations: What were some of the study's flaws as well as threats to internal and external validity?

Confounding variables:

What were the surprise variables that impacted the results?

What does this study add to my lit review?

What type of perspective does it offer to the variables?

Which chapters does this article fit?

Where does this source belong in the document?

Which other sources connect with this study?

How does this challenge or support other empirical data?

Miscellaneous notes.

Theoretical Juicer

Theoretical models also need a critical evaluation. The fact that a bigwig generates a theory does not mean it is perfect and free of gaps. Like empirical research, you need to examine the theories with care. Keep in mind that the model was developed based on someone's perspective, his or her experiences, and the data derived from that particular sample. It does not mean that the theory cannot be challenged. This form should guide you through the process of reviewing non-experimental references (e.g., articles, book chapters, and books) to pull out and discuss key content for the lit review.

Full reference: As per the sixth edition of the *Publication Manual of the American Psychological Association* (APA, 2010).

Fundamental principles: What are the components of the model?

Strengths: What works about this model?

Limitations: What is missing from this model?

Recommendations:

What does this model need in order for it to feel complete?

What does this study add to my Literature Review?

What type of perspective does it offer regarding the variables?

Which chapters does this article fit?

Which other sources connect with this study?

Miscellaneous notes.

CHAPTER KILLERS

Literature Review Chapter Killers

You are begging the Committee Members for revisions if you do any of the following:

- Write in first person instead of third person.
- Share your opinion.
- Omit references.
- Use too many direct quotes.
- Discuss the sources like an annotated bibliography rather than a synthesis of the literature.
- Do not connect the literature review contents to the variables. Sounds strange, but yes, I have seen this done before.
- Talk in circles, go off on tangents, and include stuff that does not make sense.
- Plagiarize.

The Literature Review will take a great deal of time and patience, since it involves research and writing. It is a huge challenge for many, but it will help you design the right study to collect the data you need to answer the research questions.

The next dissertation chapter is the Methodology, the process of the data collection itself. The Methodology is what is going to make your study unique from all other studies. It has many parts, so there is room for creativity and what you think is best. Read on!

ADDITIONAL HELPFUL RESOURCES

Silvia, P, (2007). *How to write a lot: A practical guide to productive academic writing.* Washington, DC: American Psychological Association.

Strunk, W., & White, E. (2000). *The elements of style* (4th ed.). Needham, MA: Allyn & Bacon.

University Writing Center—this resource is very helpful for refining your writing. Why not, since you pay lab fees for this every semester.

CHAPTER SIX

Data Scavenger Hunt: Methodology

It is now time to ask, how are you going to answer each research question? The methodology is the heart and soul of the study, the process that generates the data to answer those questions as well as support or challenge your hypotheses. What is the best way to do this? Though an experiment or working in the field? A one-shot online self-report survey or the completion of a complex set of tasks over time? The purpose of this chapter is to help you choose the right research design (context), people (participants), types of data collection items (instruments/materials), and process to do all of this (procedure) in order to answer the research questions. Table 6.1 outlines the Anatomy of a Dissertation for the Methodology.

Table 6.1 Methodology At-a-Glance from Anatomy of a Dissertation

Methodology Chapter (Chapter 3)	

Research Questions and Hypotheses	• One hypothesis per research question.	• The research questions are the foundation for the entire study.
		• They should echo each other.
		• Format so that they look like this:
		  • RQ 1:
		  • HY 1:
		  • RQ 2:
		  • HY 2:

Research Design	• Description of research design and how it was chosen for the study. • How the data will be analyzed.	• The type of study, number of groups involved. • The brief overview of the data analysis as big picture information, as opposed to detail.

Operational Definitions	• Brief definition of independent and dependent variables.
	• This definition is concrete and measurable (e.g., how much, how often, those who scored between x and y on an instrument).
	• Differs from the conceptual definition in the Literature Review, in that it is not theoretical.
Participants	• Description of participants.
	• What made them eligible for the study.
	• How they were recruited for your study.
	• Description of any compensation.
	• Provide a very clear picture of study sample.
	• Mention how you maintained their privacy.
Instruments and Materials	• Detailed description of any surveys, activities, programs, and other materials used for your study.
	• Provide a clear visual for the reader about the looks of your materials and their length of administration.

(Continued)

59

Table 6.1 Methodology At-a-Glance from Anatomy of a Dissertation (*Continued*)

Methodology Chapter (Chapter 3)

	• Rationale for using those materials. • For published instruments, should include a summary of the validation process and other psychometric properties to support robustness. • For homemade surveys, talk about the validation process to support that they will basically be "good enough" or the only option for your study.	• Surveys and other study materials belong in the Appendices. • Be confident in your explanation as to why the instrument and materials were used.
Procedure	• Detailed description of what you did when you collected the data. • Tell the reader the story from start to finish.	• The more detail, the better so that anyone could replicate your procedure to the letter.

REALITY CHECK

In order for picky consumers of research to evaluate the results of a study, the Methodology needs to be very detailed. Lack of detail in the Methodology is like not listing all of the ingredients on a food label.

WHAT TYPE OF INTERIOR (RESEARCH) DESIGN GOES WITH THOSE FOUNDATIONAL RESEARCH QUESTIONS?

The study needs to be designed to answer the research questions. Going back to our house example, how will you decorate this house (interior research design) to give it the living experience you want? The research design tells us how the study will be set up to collect the right data to answer the research questions.

The Methodology requires a great many decisions and much attention to detail. This is where the guidance of the Committee is very helpful. I always tell my students to meditate, but not to obsess because their ideas tend to not flow out as well. I want to hear their initial ideas and help them create a doable and measurable study for their allotted time frame.

CORE NUTS AND BOLTS OF RESEARCH DESIGN

There are a multitude of models to help you design all types of research experiments. Following are brief descriptions of the common research design models (Campbell & Stanley, 1963; Creswell, 2009).

- Experimental design tests the impact of relationships by random assignment for the treatment and control groups, also known as independent variables. For example, we could look at the differences in results from randomized groups: Group A (one study condition), Group B (another study condition), and Group C, the control group (no study conditions). For instance, for a study to evaluate cigarette smoking cessation interventions, we could look at the different interventions and the number of people who either quit or reduced the amount of cigarettes they smoke per day. We could randomly assign our participants to three different intervention conditions such as a smoking cessation skills class, a smoking cessation support group, and no exposure to skills or support group and measure the number of people who either quit smoking or decreased the number of cigarettes they smoke per day.

- Quasi-experimental designed studies do not have randomized groups since they have intentional assignment to different study groups. The different types of treatment groups are the independent variables. For example, years ago, I conducted a study that measured hostility level in incarcerated men from three different types of custody conditions: general population (inmates from a full security cell), inmates from a partially secured cell, and inmates in a work release program, where they slept in jail and went to work in society. The treatment conditions were already established based on the individual inmate's sentence.

- Cross-sectional studies collect data at one point in time, either on a specifically scheduled or randomly assigned date. For a dissertation, collecting one round of data at one time tends to work well.

- Longitudinal data track the participants for an allotted time span. Data are collected at various times throughout the study period, usually at the beginning, end, and several times during the middle of the research, depending on the study length and purpose. I do not recommend a longitudinal study for a dissertation or thesis. The longer the study, the more time and tuition you get to spend as a student.

- Ethnographic research takes an anthropological approach since the real world (i.e., field) becomes the laboratory. It is an extensive study that uses a multitude of data collection sources to create a clear, vivid case study to learn more about a culture or system. For instance, if we wanted to learn more about perception of neighborhood safety, we would spend time in a community, observing neighborhood activity and talking to people. The data would be used to create interventions to improve the neighborhood's sense of safety.

- Case study uses a study sample that consists of one individual ($n = 1$) or group that is intensely researched in great depth. For example, if we wanted to do a single-subject design on how a high-risk youth evolved into a gold medal Olympian, we would delve into and examine aspects of his or her life to learn about the variables that influenced his or her process.

- Meta-analysis is used to evaluate findings from multiple studies that measured the same construct. Research findings from previous studies are aggregated and analyzed together for additional patterns or findings in the data (Glass, 1976). If you wanted to do a meta-analysis on successful resilience programs for inner city youth, you would examine all data from the specific studies and their variables to draw a conclusion.

THE PEOPLE HELPING YOU DO IT: THE PARTICIPANT SAMPLE

The sample consists of the people who participate in the dissertation study through voluntary time, energy, and information. Going back to the research questions, it is time to consider who the best people are to help you answer those questions. It depends on the study. If you are studying the social networking habits of college students, then college students are the ideal participants for your sample. If you are studying the social networking habits of adults, then you need a sample from a larger age range, rather than traditionally younger aged college students, in order to generalize to the global adult population. As a journal editor, I can tell you that trying to generalize data from one specific group to the global adult population is an automatic revise and resubmit. Sometimes we cannot afford to be picky, so use a convenience sample, with participants recruited because they are an easy group to obtain data from. The main issue with convenience samples is that they tend to be homogeneous. There are many studies that use homogeneous samples. Study participants who are more alike than diverse will not necessarily ruin the study, but when interpreting and reporting the data, you need to acknowledge that the participants might have come from the same perspective. Take the results for what they are, and eventually mention it as a limitation in the discussion.

Your dissertation study might help participants on several different levels, but more often than not, you need them more than they need you. That is why you have to treat them with the utmost Integrity, Respect, and Empathy. Ideally, participation in this study is a win/win, because you need a sample and your data or intervention program might benefit the participants. Here are a few suggestions on treating the participants with Integrity:

- Be clear and honest about any risks associated with the study. For instance, for a study that requires exercise activity, the physical what-if's that come with that particular exercise would have to be clearly stated in the consent form (more about this in Chapter 7).

- Always give your respondents the option of not answering a question or withdrawing participation at any time. If you cannot use their data, so be it. It happens to the best of us!
- Maintain participants' anonymity and confidentiality.
- Leave your opinion and bias out of the study because it could influence participants' behavior and answer choices.
- Be honest about the time commitments associated with the study.
- Organize and structure each minute with participants so their time is not wasted.
- Follow through on your promises. If you promise to compensate your participants, give them what they expect.
- Do not treat people like lab rats. It is not nice, and participants will pick up on it.
- Most important, do not forget that you need them more than they need you.

There are moral and ethical standards put in place by the Institutional Review Board (IRB) and other federal regulations that need to be followed. These are outlined in Chapter 7, such as confidentiality of data, what to include in your consent form, and standards when using minors or other high-risk (e.g., physical or mental limitations, incarcerated, and pregnant) participants.

REALITY CHECK

Keep in mind that research participants might not always tell the truth, which does not mean they lack Integrity. This is known as *social desirability*—respondents lie when asked questions in order to make themselves look good or feel better about themselves (Fowler, 1995), meaning they do not want to admit to themselves or you that they feel or behave a certain way.

Proposal Versus Final Write-Up

> As in the Introduction chapter, be sure to use future tense for the proposal and past tense for the final write-up.

A detailed description of the recruitment process for the participants needs to be included in the Methodology chapter. The sample size will depend on the Committee's preference. They may want you to do a power analysis (Cohen, 1982), a statistical analysis that scientifically determines the sample size (see Additional Helpful Resources at the end of this chapter), or they might have a specific number of individuals or groups in mind. The IRB will ask you about this on their application, so most likely this section can be cut and pasted from the chapter right into the application. The description of the recruitment process should include:

- *The criteria that made the sample eligible for participation.* Were they from a specific or random group?
- *The process used to recruit the sample.* If flyers were posted around a college campus, discuss where they were posted and the rationale for those locations. Include a flyer in the appendixes of the dissertation proposal and final write-up.
- *Information about compensation.* Describe how people were rewarded for participating in the study. Course credits, gift cards, raffled items, food, and cash are the most common items used to compensate research participants.
- *Permission from each social networking site administrator to advertise, recruit, or post anything about the study.* Introductory e-mails and postings related to the study belong in the

appendixes. Do not leave anybody out; if you plan to send your survey to six separate social media groups, permission from each of the six groups will be necessary.

STUDY PROPS: INSTRUMENTS AND MATERIALS

The instruments and materials need to be directly linked to the research questions. Whether you create your own questions and items for surveys, questionnaires, interviews, focus groups, and observation protocols or use something that already exists, they need to be connected to the research questions so the data can answer them.

Qualitative, Quantitative, or Mixed Methods?

REALITY CHECK

Are you trying to learn something new (qualitative) or confirm what is already there (quantitative)?

The research design models discussed earlier in this chapter are the paradigm for the data collection process. Data collection strategies will be qualitative, quantitative, or a combination of both (mixed methods), depending on what will best answer the research questions.

- Qualitative studies are created to establish a construct's meaning and process through new data via participants' words, ideas, or products (e.g., artwork, essays). Qualitative data are original words or behaviors used to identify trends to build a theory.
- Quantitative studies collect data in an attempt to learn about and validate an existing construct or program.

Quantitative survey responses have some type of fixed
choice, which can easily be coded into numbers, if they
are not already numerical, to perform statistical analyses or frequency analyses, which is the head count and
percentage of how many people responded this way or
that (i.e., strongly disagreed, disagreed, agreed, strongly
agreed) per survey item. These studies take a scientific
approach since the numerical data can provide evidence
for the variables.

* Mixed methods encompasses both qualitative and quantitative data collection strategies, since data are collected from respondents' words and also numbers. The
research questions will determine if you need mixed-
method strategies. For example, a survey could ask for
open responses on items that invite people to comment
freely as well as include a numerical rating scale, so they
can evaluate what is already there.

Table 6.2 presents a variety of different options for data
collection strategies.

I learned through the years that qualitative items are easier to develop, but organizing, analyzing, and possibly scoring people's words or work require a lot of time and Energy.
The good news is that there are several software options out
there to help with the process. Quantitative items are the
opposite, in that they need a great deal of work that involves
many rounds of extensive review and edits to develop strong
item stems (survey questions) and relevant response choices.
So if there are standardized questionnaire or tests available,
that might be a good option, since it might not make sense to
reinvent the wheel. A good source to consult for a standardized instrument is the *The Mental Measurements Yearbook* (see,
e.g., Spies, Carlson, & Geisinger, 2010), which can be found
in most university or college libraries.

Table 6.2 Quickie Chart for Data Collection Strategies

Data Collection Method	Brief Description	Pros	Cons	Notes	Qualitative, Quantitative, or Mixed-Methods?
Interviews (individual)	Hear and learn individual insight to build a theory.	• Potential data are rich and inclusive. • Less participants needed. • Builds a relationship with interviewee. • There are several interview models to help guide the process.	• Interviewee might not share valuable insight. • Might require skillful facilitation to keep interviewee on track.	• Be mindful of time. • Send thank you note after the interview. • Stick to interview questions. • Build and maintain trust with interviewee.	Qualitative
Questionnaire and surveys (open ended items)	Gain individual insight from their written words.	• Potential data are rich and inclusive. • Can be administered online or on paper.	• Respondents might not answer because they do not feel like writing. • Respondents go off on tangents and do not answer the question. • If handwritten, deciphering people's handwriting can be quite a challenge.	• Make sure the items are well written so that respondents know what they are being asked. • Only include the exact number of questions necessary so respondents do not get bored.	Qualitative

(Continued)

Table 6.2 Quickie Chart for Data Collection Strategies *(Continued)*

Data Collection Method	Brief Description	Pros	Cons	Notes	Qualitative, Quantitative, or Mixed-Methods?
Questionnaire and surveys (closed response questions)	Validate a theo-retical model or construct from items that are easily coded into numbers.	• Assess large group of respondents. • Data are relatively easy to organize and analyze. • Can be administered online or on paper. • For online question-naires, the data's spreadsheet is set up automatically. • Participants need not disclose identity, which may lead to more honest answers.	• Organizing the data and hand-entering it on a spreadsheet for paper-based surveys can be time-consuming. • Background in statis-tics or a statistician friend is needed to help analyze and inter-pret the data.	• Always tell respondents about the amount of time it takes to com-plete the survey. • Do not write items that could offend people.	Quantitative

| Focus groups (group interviews) | Structured and open-ended interviews of multiple people at the same time. | • Gain individual responses from multiple people.
• The group dynamic might inspire responses.
• Saves time, since you get individual responses in "bulk," rather than through individual interviews. | • Respondents might either be quiet or not completely honest due to the group dynamic and social desirability.
• Very time-consuming to write questions, facilitate group, and analyze the data.
• Notes or your recording have to be perfectly clear; I do not suggest you attempt to remember everything said. | • Have experience with focus group facilitation; manage the group's input level by managing the overly talkative and quiet group members.
• There are certifications to be focus group moderator.
• Be aware of any politics within group members, which could influence the data.
• Either a second person or a tape recorder is needed to take copious notes or record the session.
• Have food—it tends to draw people out, make them feel like they got something for their time.
• Organizing and analyzing the data can be time-consuming. | Qualitative |

(Continued)

Table 6.2 Quickie Chart for Data Collection Strategies *(Continued)*

Data Collection Method	Brief Description	Pros	Cons	Notes	Qualitative, Quantitative, or Mixed-Methods?
Observation	Intensely watch people's behavior in either a laboratory or participants' natural environment (field).	• Excellent way to learn a great deal about individual, group, and system behavior.	• Need multiple observations so that people get used to observers and act naturally to avoid Hawthorne Effect (Adair, 1984), the tendency for people to act differently under observation.	• Create a rubric or scoring system to guide observation or watch freely and take notes on what is seen. • Blend in and be as minimally invasive as possible.	Mixed methods
Benchmarking	To compare a process or system to other processes and systems.	• Learn more about what other people are actually doing. • Can do this by interviewing, Internet research, or through field observation.	• Systems, groups, or organizations might be forbidden to share information.	• Could create a rubric or other rating system to guide the comparison. • Be mindful of the similarities and differences of the systems that you are comparing.	Mixed methods

Document review	To evaluate work, reports, or journals, such as portfolios.	• Looking at end products	• Participants could feel judged and get insulted.	• Plan to create rubrics or a standardized rating system to make subjective work objective.	Mixed methods
Scores from standardized instruments	Use of data from instruments with evidence of reliability and validity, such as educational test scores, personality tests, and other standardized measures.	• The data from a measure with a high level of credibility can be valuable to a study.	• Consider issues like text anxiety as well as the environment when evaluating test scores, so view them with a critical eye.	• Know the test and the meaning of the score inside and out.	Quantitative

I have found that technology makes data collection significantly easier. Since there are more devices available and easier access to the Internet than in the dial-up days, online surveys are becoming a more practical choice than pencil-and-paper surveys. I use them whenever I can to avoid hand entering or scanning in the data, and it is easy to sample a truly global population because the survey can be sent in a link via e-mail. There are several choices of online survey hosts, with different levels of memberships, from free with limited use to fees associated with unlimited use. The type of membership depends on the needs of your study. Check to see if your program or department has a license or contract with one that you might be able to use.

Once the data are entered and ready to analyze through a computer program (e.g., SPSS or SAS) to give you the statistics you need, the right statistical test will be chosen based on the research question. You have to tell it how to perform the analyses, so a background in stats or a good statistician friend nearby is necessary for interpreting and deciphering the results. You will have to know and be able to explain all your results to your committee, whether you ran them yourself or someone did it for you. It is essential that you know what the numbers mean.

Creating survey items, interview questions, and scoring systems is not an easy task, described by Payne (1951) as an art and science. The goal for the items is that they are clear and easy to understand by respondents. Here are simple item and question to-do's:

- Ask one question at a time.
- Make items as short as possible.

REALITY CHECK

Here are the differences in time commitments between qualitative and quantitative studies. Qualitative, open-ended items take less time to review, finalize, and validate, but more time is spent organizing and analyzing the data. Quantitative, closed-ended items take longer to review, finalize, and validate, but organizing and analyzing the data takes significantly less time. Sometimes qualitative data can be very subjective and may need a little objectivity, like portfolios, conversation, as well as observations, so a rubric or other scoring tool might be necessary. All in all, both are a lot of work, but with qualitative, the bulk of the work is on the back end, whereas with quantitative, the workload is heavier on the front end.

- Eliminate bias or your opinion so that you do not influence the respondent's answer choice.
- Watch for redundancy in the items. Sometimes it makes sense to ask the same question many different ways and, in other instances, it seems repetitive and annoying, depending on the purpose of the study. For the layman, surveys should be as to-the-point as possible.
- Match the item stem or question to the response choices (Likert rating, check all that apply, rank order, etc.), so that they fit.
- Avoid providing a middle response when asking respondents to take a stance (e.g., strongly disagree, disagree, agree, strongly agree). The data might seem wishy-washy and not answer the research question.
- For rating items, use 1 for the lower as opposed to the higher ranking. It is less confusing for respondents.

- Keep in mind that the data collected from the items should help answer the research question.
- Pilot the items to make sure they "work."

REALITY CHECK

The instrument should be user friendly as well as written clearly and simply enough that most adults can quickly and easily go through the items.

All data collection tools need to provide evidence of validity and reliability through application of psychometric best practices. You might not do everything to address the best practices of psychometrics, but you have to test out the items—whether they are survey items, test questions, interviews, or focus groups—to make sure they work.

REALITY CHECK

A thermometer is an instrument. You know it is valid because it only measures temperature, which is what it intends to measure. It has proven to be reliable because it consistently measures temperature. Data collection in all forms should follow that same principle. It needs to measure what it is supposed to measure, every time it is used.

CONSTRUCT VALIDITY

Samuel Messick is the father of construct validity. His seminal model, Unified Notion of Construct Validity, helps us look at our instrument from all angles to confirm that it will accurately measure the constructs and variables (Messick,

1995). Keep the following in mind for choosing data collection tools: They need to be tried and true to ensure that they are going to get you the data needed to answer the research questions. Just as we know that our dependable thermometer will always accurately read our body temperature, we need to know that our dissertation data collection tools will give us the right information, but that does not necessarily mean it will be what we want to hear. However, at least we know it is correct. Here are the summarized six components of Messick's model, which are all interconnected:

1. Content validity ensures the appropriateness of the instrument's items, that they are clearly worded and represent the construct. Item reviews from content experts help ensure that we did not leave out anything important or include something that does not fit.
2. Substantive validity considers the whole instrument from the items, and format, to the scoring system. Piloting the instrument on a sample population could help us see which items are skipped or misunderstood.
3. Structural validity endorses the accuracy of the instrument's scoring system by comparing instrument data to real or actual (concurrent) behavior. For instance, if Mr. Miserable scores high on your happiness instrument, the items and scoring system might have to be readjusted.
4. Generalizability ensures that the instrument's pilot sample is representative of the intended respondent population. It is ideal to have typical respondents of the instrument on its development team.
5. External validity in this context is how well the instrument under development correlates with other similar (convergent) or different (divergent) instruments or behavior. For example, if you were creating an instrument

on anxiety, scores from this pilot should be closely related to scores from other anxiety measures and different from scores that assess for patience.

6. Consequential validity evaluates the meaning of an instrument's results. This considers how the data impact individuals, groups, and organizations by asking, "What does it really mean if this person scored high in one dimension and low in another dimension?"

I joke in my classes that if the first draft and final version of the instrument's items look completely different and you are extremely sick of looking at it, then it is almost ready to launch. My surveys always have multiple draft phases for item writing, first being reviewed by content experts, followed by survey experts, and then by members of the participant sample. These reviews help us ensure that we do not make errors of omission, leaving out important survey items, and commission, items that are irrelevant. Although validity and reliability can be two entirely separate books, here are a few tips to ensure validity and reliability:

- Data collection tools are extensively reviewed and refined based on feedback by multiple sets of eyes from various study stakeholders such as the Chair, the Committee Members, sample population representatives, colleagues in your program class, content experts, and people who do not know your topic. These reviews confirm that the items or questions are clear.
- Interview a small sample of typical respondents on the instrument and items to confirm appropriateness.
- Pilot the instrument or program on a small group of sample participants.
- Correlate and compare results from the instrument to other instruments or data collection methods that assess

similar (convergent) and different (divergent) constructs. For instance, if you created an instrument on anxiety, you could administer and correlate the results from other anxiety tests and depression inventories, since they are similar and responses should be similar, as well as a happiness measure, which should show opposing responses because it is a different construct.

- Conduct statistics such as Cronbach's alpha, correlations, and factor analyses on quantitative instruments. Additional references for this can be found in the Additional Helpful Resources section at the end of this chapter.

Go Get It: Study Procedure

The Procedure is each step in the study's data collection process. This is what you did to collect your data. This section needs to be as detailed as possible. I always went by my Chair's rule of thumb, which was that a good Procedure section needs to be detailed to the point that if you mysteriously disappeared before you collected your data, someone else could carry your study through, your way. This has been my gold standard for evaluating methodologies for years in all of my research roles. This is also where empathy is important, putting ourselves in the shoes of our participants in order to make the process as user friendly as possible for all involved.

You need to be very transparent and describe exactly what you are doing with the participants to confirm that your study is ethical and relevant. Following are the people who care about the Procedure and why:

- *The Committee.* They want to confirm that you are using the most rigorous methodology possible to collect your data. They care about this study and are there to help you make the study the best it can be.

79

- *IRB.* They want to ensure that you are treating the participants with the highest codes of ethics and standards, as well as maintaining confidentiality, anonymity, and Integrity.
- *Group, organization, and system where you are going to collect your data.* They need to be reassured that you are not wasting their time and that the purpose of your study aligns with their mission statement and research agenda.

Thus, do not skimp on the level of detail. If you are going to be obsessive about detail, it should be in the Methodology chapter. However, it also needs to be extremely focused and obviously honest. Do not ramble to fill up space, but know that you need to tell the whole story. In terms of formatting, this detailed step-by-step Procedure needs to be in paragraph form and written in the third person. For dissertations, vague Methodologies often result in revisions from the Committee and the IRB. Therefore, take your time and write this section so you can be transparent to stakeholders about the Procedure.

Proposal Versus Write-Up

As a reminder, the dissertation or thesis proposal must be written it in the future tense because you are proposing the study and the data are not collected. The final write-up will be written in past tense since it was already done.

What Type of Detail Needs to Be in the Procedure?

- Step by step of the participants' experiences. For the final write-up, tell exactly what they did while they participated in your study.

- The average amount of time for all parts of the methodology. Whether it was a training, intervention, activity, or completing a survey, how much time did everything take?
- Process of gaining their consent before study participation.

CHAPTER KILLERS

Methodology Chapter Killers

You are begging Committee Members for revisions if you do any of the following:

- Describe the methodology in first person. Use third person instead, which is consistent throughout the dissertation/thesis, unless otherwise specified in your department.
- Vague descriptions of the methodology. You need to clearly communicate this very important process.
- The research design does not match up to the research questions. All parts of the study should be connected to the variables, so do not go all over the place.
- Not changing verb tenses from the future to past in the proposal and final dissertation write-ups.
- Neither validate a homemade instrument nor discuss the validation process for one that is published and standardized.
- Use a sample size that is too small.
- Seem biased either for or against your participants.

Designing and delivering a study requires a great deal of detail and decisions. You should now have a dissertation study proposal signed. Before you begin any research activities, study activities need approval from the IRB.

81

ADDITIONAL HELPFUL RESOURCES

Campbell, D., & Stanley, J. (1963). *Experimental and quasi-experimental designs for research.* Boston, MA: Houghton Mifflin.

Creswell, J. (2009). *Research design: Qualitative, quantitative, and mixed methods approaches* (3rd ed.). Thousand Oaks, CA: Sage.

Fowler, F. (1995). *Improving survey questions: Design and evaluation.* Thousand Oaks, CA: Sage.

Spies, R. A., Carlson, J. F., & Geisinger, K. F. (Eds.), *The eighteenth mental measurements yearbook.* Lincoln: University of Nebraska Press.

CHAPTER SEVEN

The Institutional
Review Board (IRB)

The Institutional Review Board (IRB) is a federally mandated committee whose role is to ensure that all human research participants are treated with the highest ethical standards of respect, safety, and fairness (Eissenberg et al., 2004). Universities and colleges, as well as most other large institutions, such as hospitals and school districts, have an IRB or similar committee to approve research studies that involve human subjects. Most IRBs have a website with policies, applications, submission information, and templates for consent forms. Since a majority of dissertations in the social sciences use human participants, you will have to go through the IRB application process to gain approval in order to start all data collection activities.

In the university or college setting, the IRB committee usually consists of two to five faculty members and administrators. There are different levels of review, depending on the nature of the study. For example, a study that asks participants to exercise and immediately complete a depression test might need a full committee review, where each IRB member needs to thoroughly evaluate the methodology to understand the treatment of human participants in the study. In this case, the IRB would want to confirm that the participants show evidence that they are physically healthy enough to carry through the study's activities, participants are fully aware of the study's risks and benefits, and the study is conducted in a safe manner, such as distributing water to participants and giving them the option to drop out of the study at any time. On a different level, a study that surveys people on their attitudes about learning new computer software might be exempt (excused) from full board review and evaluated by only one person, since there are no risks associated with that type of study. Each individual university or college IRB might have their own levels of review and accompanying documents.

THE IRB APPLICATION PROCESS

IRBs typically require a certification through completion of a brief training course that is found online or in a workshop. The training generally highlights best practices in research using human participants. Your department and Committee will most likely be familiar with the IRB mandates at your university or college. At the end of the training, you will receive a certificate to include in the IRB application.

The application itself is typically very straightforward. The questions are mostly about the methodology such as the participant recruitment process and materials (e.g., e-mails or flyers that advertise study and solicit participation), participant criteria and characteristics, instruments and materials, and study procedure, as well as the study purpose and intended use of data. The good news is that this information can be cut and pasted directly from the Introduction and Methodology chapters of your dissertation proposal, which are written in future tense.

REALITY CHECK

The IRB process is similar to filing for a work permit when you do home improvement. Your city or township really does not care what type of project you do, as long as it adheres to the residential safety codes. The IRB is similar in that they do not really care what type of study you are doing, as long as you treat your research participants with a very high level of Integrity (see Chapter 6) and are mindful of the IRB Four.

THE IRB FOUR: VOLUNTARY, ANONYMITY, CONFIDENTIALITY, AND TRANSPARENCY

Just like the city or town inspector who evaluates construction projects to confirm that project elements (e.g., electric, plumbing) comply with safety codes, the IRB has its own standards for human participation. Following are the main priorities of the IRB, which I refer to as the IRB Four:

1. *Voluntary.* People's participation in which their time, Energy, expertise, data, honest answers, and demonstration of behaviors are of their free will and without any obligations. This means no begging, bribing, bullying, or manipulating people into study participation, as well as allowing people to quit their participation at any time, without any hassle or judgment.
2. *Anonymity.* Participants' identity is completely omitted or separated from their data. Individual opinions, test scores, or other performance indicators will not be

directly linked to a name. Both qualitative and quantitative sample data are condensed and analyzed together to look for patterns and trends. For a single-subject design, the participant or group is given an alias.

3. *Confidentiality*. Researchers keep the data collection process and data itself private and only share anonymous and aggregated data with written consent of the participants or parents or guardians for minors. For educational research done in a school setting with minors, the Family Educational Rights and Privacy Act (FERPA) protects the identities of students by requiring written permission from parents or guardians for anyone to view students' school records. Go to their website (www2.ed.gov/policy/gen/guid/fpco/ferpa/index.html) for more information on this.

4. *Transparency*. Full disclosure of any consequences from research participation, such as risks and benefits. Risks include any potential side effects or discomforts from study participation. For instance, in a study that asks participants to eat chocolate, the risks associated with chocolate consumption might be excessive calorie intake and an increased heart rate from the sugar. These are not hazardous health risks, but certainly potential consequences of eating chocolate that should be disclosed. A large portion of studies in the social sciences, where participants are asked to self-report attitudes or behaviors, are able to say "there are no risks associated with this study" to answer that question. Benefits from study participation include free services and increased knowledge in the study's topic. For instance, if the study asked people to attend educational classes on financial responsibility, the participants might learn facts and skills to

manage and save money, which would be useful and relevant to improving their lives.

SOLID CONSENT FORMS

All human research participants must consent (signed by parents or guardians for minors) to being in a research study prior to their involvement. A signature is usually needed for face-to-face activities and verbal consent for data collection by phone. Online research activities normally ask that participants go to a website, read the consent form, and click "agree" to gain access to the study. Consent forms are kept separate from data to ensure anonymity.

Overall, consent forms should be detailed, without being overly wordy. Most IRBs have a template for consent forms on their websites. Following is a list of the generic information needed in a solid consent form:

- Title of study.
- Your name and contact information.
- Name of your department and university or college.
- Your Chairperson's name and contact information.
- IRB representative's name and contact information.
- One or two sentences about the purpose of the study.
- Description of what makes the participants eligible for the study or why they were recruited.
- Brief summary of research activities (i.e., what you are asking them to do).
- Mention of time commitment for study activities.
- Risks associated with the study.
- Benefits associated with the study.
- Thank you for your participation!

REALITY CHECK

If you plan to use minors or people with physical, psychological, or legal restrictions, such as people who are incarcerated or have mental illnesses, budget extra time into your Realistic Work Schedule, since these groups are considered to be special needs participants. You will most likely have to provide additional paperwork to the IRB to prove how you are taking extra care in working with them, which might take more time to review.

IRB SURVIVAL SKILLS

Maintaining your cool, especially with the IRB, is an essential part of gaining approval. Sometimes the IRB process can be long and painful, with the threat of potential revisions. Given that this can be a stressful piece of the dissertation experience, it is essential to remain emotionally intelligent (revisit The Top 10 Rules for Maintaining Emotional and Social Intelligence in Chapter 1).

Following are some tips to keep moving forward when going through the IRB process:

- Tell them what they want to know so they understand the nature of all research activities.
- Do not push back on any of the revisions; the faster you give them what they want, the sooner your study will be approved.
- Turn in the IRB application and supporting documents as soon as data collection activities and instruments are approved by the Committee.
- Submit revisions the way you would for the Committee — either a memo or spreadsheet with each revision, the

changes made, and the page number in the document where it is located. The easier you make it for them to review the revisions, the quicker they might review your application and return it to you.

- Make use of the downtime since you can neither contact participants nor start any data collection activities without approval. The downtime is a good opportunity to work on other parts of the dissertation such as the Literature Review and prep for the data collection activities (e.g., make spreadsheets, buy supplies, make contacts). However, I do not suggest that you photocopy anything like a paper survey until you are officially approved by the IRB, just in case they suggest even a minor change.
- Politely follow up if the wait seems excessive (each individual IRB will vary; check with others who have been approved), but do not stalk them.

Now that you have received your official approval letter from the IRB, it is time to collect data. This is the fun part, because you are actually following through on your dissertation proposal by conducting your own study and collecting original data. Remember, YOU CAN DO IT!

CHAPTER EIGHT

Making Sense of the Data Collection Scavenger Hunt: Results

Great job on collecting data for your dissertation study! You did it! Now it is time to organize and analyze the freshly collected data before they age and become outdated or yesterday's news. The Results chapter, typically Chapter 4, is where you present the study's actual data, which are typically structured and presented in order of research questions (Pyrczak & Bruce, 2000). The research questions and hypotheses are restated, followed by the data that answer that research question. Since the purpose of the study is to answer each research question, only relevant data that answer the research question need to be presented. Other interesting data might come out from the study, outside the realm of the research questions. You can report these data in a section for Additional Analyses that succeeds the Analysis of Research Questions and Hypotheses or can be saved for another study or article.

The Results chapter is where you present and summarize the aggregated data. Readers of your study need a clear picture of the results so they can form their own interpretations (Cone & Foster, 2006). Picky consumers of research will notice if something is missing and bring it to your attention. The Results chapter should include a brief Introduction, Demographics, Analysis of Research Questions, and Hypotheses, and Additional Analysis. Deciding whether to attach raw data will vary per Committee, but if you do, it belongs in the appendixes. Table 8.1 explains what goes into this chapter.

DATA SPEAK

The Results chapter starts with a brief introduction that summarizes the methodology to give the reader a background of the research design, number of participants, instruments and measures used, as well as how data were collected and analyzed. This is usually a paragraph or two (at most) to set the stage for the study findings.

Next, the demographic variables are presented, such as gender, age groups, number of people per treatment group, or other relevant background information. Demographic variables are usually presented by the number of people and their percentages for each group, also known as frequency analyses. For example, "out of the 100 participants, there were $n = 60$ women (60%) and 40 men (40%)." Data are also reported by

Table 8.1 Results Chapter At-a-Glance From Anatomy of a Dissertation

	Results Chapter (Chapter 4)	
Chapter Subsection	**Should Include**	**Points to Remember**
Introduction	• Brief summary of the purpose of the study and method. • Description of the process or application for data analysis.	• Short, sweet, and to the point. • Just say what you did to analyze it.
Descriptive Demographic Data	• Frequency analyses of number and percentage of relevant demographic groups (e.g., gender, age group, nationality, etc.).	• You do not have to include any SPSS codes. • You may have a table for this.
Analysis of Research Questions and Hypotheses	• Each research question and hypothesis with a table or figure of the data that either supports or challenges the hypothesis. • Brief mention whether it supports or challenges the research cited in the literature review.	• Write statistics in proper format (see statistical chart in Appendix A) • Eliminate bias; the data should be unfolded and connected very objectively. • Tell it like it is. • Don't skimp on the real evidence.

(Continued)

Table 8.1 Results Chapter At-a-Glance From Anatomy of a Dissertation (Continued)

	Results Chapter (Chapter 4)	
Chapter Subsection	**Should Include**	**Points to Remember**
Additional Analyses	• Other observations or patterns in your data that you find is worth mentioning. • Brief mention on how it fits into the literature.	• Write statistics in proper format (see statistical chart in Appendix A). • Eliminate bias; the data should be unfolded and connected very objectively. • Tell it like it is. • Don't skimp on the real evidence.

the means (averages), standard deviations (statistical term for give or take), and their percentages. For example, "the $M = 19$ years and the $SD = 1$ year, which accounted for 80% of the sample." In other words, the average age of respondents was 19, give or take a year (meaning a number participants were 18 or 20 as well). You can easily calculate demographic data through Microsoft Excel or SPSS, a statistical program. Data might be also presented by mode (the most popular age group) or median (the center of the data set). This depends on the preference of your Committee. Personally, I prefer to report means.

The Results chapter (Demographic, Analysis of Research Questions and Hypotheses, and Additional Analyses) includes tables, figures (i.e., charts and graphs), and more writing. The number of tables and figures should depend the study's needs. My rule of thumb for tables and figures is that they should be used to help tell the story, but not overused so that it feels like wasted space. All tables and figures should have text to explain the meaning of the numbers. The *Publication Manual of the American Psychological Association*, 6th edition (APA, 2010), explains how the different tables and figures should be presented, according to the data type and statistic. Larger tables and figures usually belong in the appendixes, so they do not disrupt the flow of text for the reader. The Committee can give you preferences and feedback about which tables and figures you need.

Following the demographic section is the Analysis of Research Questions, where the data are read objectively and linked to their research questions and hypotheses. The research questions and hypotheses are presented in the same way as in Methodology, typically in the following format:

Presenting Analyses of Research Questions and Hypotheses

RQ1:

HY1:

Tables, figures, and text that includes:

* The data to answer the research question.
* Whether the data challenged or supported the hypothesis.
* How the data challenged or supported previous research.

RQ2:

HY2:

Each research question and hypothesis should follow the same format.

The statistical test is chosen to directly answer the research question. For example, if your research question was "How do relationship status, personality traits, and employment status impact Facebook satisfaction level?" you are investigating how several independent variables correlate with one dependent variable, so a multiple regression analysis would be applied.

Reporting data should be factual and not biased; you are answering each research question by telling it like it is with the relevant data. Do not worry if you do not find statistical significance; you are not graded on the data outcome, just how well you explain it. In this chapter, no matter how tempting, neither interpret the data nor try to make sense of it; save that for your Discussion chapter. You might want to succinctly indicate whether it challenges or supports your hypotheses, theoretical models, or other empirical data. This explanation is usually brief, since it is talked about at length

---

REALITY CHECK

Presenting data is usually right to the point: "The data said this (insert statistic) and that (insert statistic), which supports So-and-So's (year) work that found . . .

---

in the discussion, where you get to share your thoughts on the data.

There might be data that come out of your study that seem worth noting but do not neatly fit under the realm of the Analysis of Research Questions and Hypotheses. These data belong under Additional Analyses or in your next article and should use the same stick-to-the-point guidelines as the Analysis of Research Questions and Hypotheses.

Regardless of the type of data, I highly recommend that you set up a way to organize the data before data collection begins. A good time to do this is while you are waiting for IRB approval, so that you keep moving forward. You want to be ready for all the rich data that will hopefully tell you what you want to know.

WHAT DO I DO WITH THESE NUMBERS?

Survey, observation, and secondary data (e.g., test scores) can be forms of numerical and forced-choice responses. The data should be analyzed via an appropriate statistic to match the research questions. According to Urdan (2010), statistics allow researchers to get a sense of what is typical and common from large groups of people. These data need to be organized onto a spreadsheet before any type of analysis. For paper-based surveys, the data will have to be hand entered or scanned into the spreadsheet. I highly recommend using Microsoft Excel to build your spreadsheet, since statistical software programs like SPSS and SAS will read Excel. Most university and college libraries and computer labs are stocked with these software packages. When I was in grad school, my tight budget wouldn't allow SPSS. For my dissertation, I did quantitative paper surveys that were hand entered into Excel, saved on a disk, and taken to the campus computer lab so I could analyze the stats on SPSS, since there was no online surveying at that time.

Online survey data typically will easily convert into a choice of spreadsheet formats, including Excel and SPSS. After the data are organized into the spreadsheet, each response option should receive a numerical value. You will code in a way that is best for your data and study. Most groups or ratings can easily be turned into numerical codes. Some common numerical coding examples are shown in Table 8.2.

Statistical writing requires proper formatting. Cone and Foster (2006) suggest that the following be included when describing your numbers:

- Name of the statistic
- Sufficient amount of data to answer the research question
- Significance values
- Sample sizes
- Effect sizes
- Means
- Standard deviations
- Clear tables and figures

See Additional Helpful Resources at the end of this chapter for additional resources about analyzing and writing up statistics as well as the *Summary Chart of Statistics, What to Report, Abbreviations, and Suggested Syntax* in Appendix A.

Table 8.2 *Common Coding Examples*

Variable	Categories and Codes
Gender	Female = 1
	Male = 2
Age groups	18–29 years = 1
	30–39 years = 2
	40–49 years = 3
	50–59 years = 4
	60–69 years = 5
	70–79 years = 6
	80 years and older = 7
Likert ratings (that are not already numerical)	Strongly Disagree = 1
	Disagree = 2
	Agree = 3
	Strongly Agree = 4
Experimental groups	Skills workshop only = 1
	Skills workshop and support group = 2
	Support group only = 3
	Control group = 4
Groups based on skills ranking	Beginner = 1
	Intermediate = 2
	Expert = 3

WHAT DO I DO WITH THE WORDS?

Open-ended data are words and phrases derived from interviews, surveys, focus groups, and observations. The amount of data will vary per participant. For example, in an open-ended survey, you might have a respondent who writes mini-essays and other people who provide one-word answers. There is nothing we can do about that—it is what it is. However, quality is more important than quantity. You might have a respondent ramble on about something and never actually answer the question. This person might be an outlier—a participant whose responses reflect experiences that are vastly different from the majority of the group. I suggest mentioning outlier data, since their insight is interesting to present alongside data from the "norm."

The data need to be organized, condensed, and analyzed to evaluate for trends and patterns through a process called a content analysis (Boyatzis, 1998). The key to a content analysis is to look for what was said most frequently to establish evidence-based themes. Although there is software out there that you can use, it is helpful to understand the steps in performing a content analysis the good old fashioned way, organized by individual open-ended items. Table 8.3 presents two examples of open-ended survey questions from five workshop participants that go through the four step content analysis process to look for patterns from the responses.

In this example, we were able to get themes. For the general strengths of the workshop, we learned that participants reported them to be the workshop materials, trainer, and topic. As far as suggestions to improve the workshop, most of the participants did not have any suggestions to improve the workshop, but a few helpful recommendations were shared.

Tips for Conducting a Content Analysis

- List each item said from each person as a single response as seen in the first column on Table 8.3.
- If something was said at least once, write it down. Once it is condensed, write a number representing the number of people who said it. You do not have to write the number one if it was only said once, as seen in the third column of Table 8.3.

Table 8.3 Content Analysis Example: Workshop Evaluation Survey

Step 1	Step 2	Step 3	Step 4
Separate for Each Survey Question Straight From the Survey ($n = 5$ Responses)	Lists of Raw Condensed Data (Unedited Statements From Individual People)	Summarize Data (Data Edited Into Similar Themes)	Condense Data Into Common Themes (Combined Data Grouped by Similar Themes)
What were the strengths of the workshop?	• The trainer was good. • The topic will help me at work. • The handouts look like they will be useful. • The case studies were interesting. • The trainer's personal examples. • The time went by fast.	• Trainer • Helpful topic • Handouts • Case studies • Teaching examples • Workshop felt short • Materials • Break from work • Learned about the topic	• Workshop materials (2) (handouts, case studies) • Trainer (2) (knowledge, teaching examples) • Workshop topic (helpful, learned from it) • Everything • Seemed fast • Break from work

(Continued)

101

Table 8.3 Content Analysis Example: Workshop Evaluation Survey (Continued)

Step 1	Step 2	Step 3	Step 4
Separate for Each Survey Question Straight From the Survey (n = 5 Responses)	Lists of Raw Condensed Data (Unedited Statements From Individual People)	Summarize Data (Data Edited Into Similar Themes)	Condense Data Into Common Themes (Combined Data Grouped by Similar Themes)
	• Good materials.	• Trainer knowledge	
	• It was a break from work.	• Everything	
	• I learned more about the topic.		
	• The trainer was knowledgeable.		
	• Everything, the workshop was excellent.		

What suggestions do you have to improve the workshop?	• Nothing. • The workshop was excellent. I wouldn't change anything. • Provide case studies that are more applicable to this group. • There should be a follow-up session for people needing to practice the skills. • None.	• No suggestions • No suggestions • Case studies need to be more applicable to the group. • Provide the option of a follow-up session for skills. • No suggestions	• No suggestions (3) • Case studies that are applicable to this group • Follow-up skills workshop

- When people are saying the same thing but using different words, pick the most common term. For instance, if you receive responses such as excellent, awesome, wonderful, and superb, you can decide on one term, such as excellent (4), and condense the data.
- When one person uses a catch phrase that might make them stick out, find a common synonym so that their data remain anonymous. For example, if only one person described something as being *groovy* and everyone else used the term *cool*, condense the "groovy" with the "cool," since they can be considered to be synonymous. If the respondents eventually see the condensed data, the person whose catchphrase is "groovy" will remain anonymous.
- Prioritize data from most to least common themes.

REALITY CHECK

To clarify the difference between the Results and Discussion chapters, the Results chapter just gives you the *what*, or the pure data itself, whereas the discussion answers the *why* question of how the data might have ended up that way.

CHAPTER KILLERS

Results Chapter Killers

You are begging Committee Members for revisions if you do any of the following:

- Omit data you collected
- Report incorrect data

- Use a statistic that does not align with the research question. For instance, if you are not comparing groups, do not use a stat like analysis of variance (ANOVA), analysis of covariance (ANCOVA), or multivariate analysis of variance (MANOVA).
- Write statistics out in the improper format.
- Interpret the data.
- Not condense qualitative data.
- Not organize data by research question.
- Not mention how the data either supported or challenged your hypothesis.
- Incorrectly use first person (unless specified).

Now that you have presented the actual data, it's time to interpret and connect your study to the real world. That is the purpose of the final chapter. Chapter 9 focuses on the Discussion, which dissects why the data came out that way and what it might mean. This is where you get to shine as the expert.

ADDITIONAL HELPFUL RESOURCES

Boyatzis, R. (1998). *Transforming qualitative information: Thematic analysis and code development.* Thousand Oaks, CA: Sage.

Cooper, H. (2011). *Reporting research in psychology: How to meet journal article reporting standards* (6th ed.). Washington, DC: American Psychological Association.

Urdan, T. (2010). *Statistics in plain English* (3rd ed.). New York, NY: Routledge.

Wetcher-Hendricks, D., (2011). *Analyzing quantitative data: An introduction for social scientists.* Hoboken, NJ: Wiley.

CHAPTER NINE

I Am Listening, Data: Discussion

Congratulations on muscling through your Results chapter! Now, you need to understand and listen to the results in order to interpret them for the Discussion chapter. Once you truly comprehend what the data in the form of numbers or words mean, then onward to the Discussion, your final dissertation chapter. Yes, I did say the final chapter, which indicates you are almost done!

I love writing discussions because this is where I get to be creative and connect my data to theory and practice. When I write a discussion, I know I am contributing to the field. You are an expert in your topic with a fresh batch of empirical data (i.e., your data), so present what you know. It can be very exciting to watch your data come to life by fitting it to the real world.

REALITY CHECK

Imagine if you had a dozen basketballs released from a net in mid-ceiling. The purpose of the Results chapter is to simply report on how and where the balls fell and how that met your hypothesis. The Discussion chapter tells the reader your position as to why the balls fell in those spots. Did it have to do with the amount of air in the balls, the breeze from the open window, length of ceiling to floor, all of the above, or none of the above? You need to provide an explanation for this.

In this chapter, you will dissect the data and provide a rationale for the results and what they mean. The Discussion chapter has several subsections, which are displayed in Table 9.1.

INTRODUCTION

This is the opener to the Discussion chapter where you transition the reader from what was done before the data are interpreted and implications are drawn. In the Introduction you provide a quick refresher (a few paragraphs at most) about how the data were collected and analyzed, without being too wordy or redundant from the Methodology or Results chapters. Yes, you do tend to repeat yourself in a dissertation at times, but think of it as rolling out the red carpet for your interpretation and implications of the findings, which are very important. Similar to the Introduction chapter, the heart of the discussion is the "what, so what, and now what" (Silberman, 1998) to explain the nature of the results as well as the study limitations, issues within the study that impact the results.

Table 9.1 Discussion Chapter At-a-Glance From Anatomy of a Dissertation

	Discussion Chapter (Chapter 5)	
Chapter Subsection	**Should Include**	**Points to Remember**
Introduction	• Very brief summary of the purpose of the study, method, and how the data were analyzed.	• Short, sweet, and to the point.
Interpretation of Findings	• Organize per research question. • Talk about the results, their meaning, their connection to the literature, and how the data could be used.	• Be creative, this is one of the fun parts.
Limitations	• Any limitations noted about the study.	• Swallow your pride and be humble; every study has them. • Be assertive.
Implications for Theory and Practice	• Your interpretation of the overall meaning of the data, as well as how it fits into the literature and "real world."	• Think of this as settling the argument in the literature. • Remember, you are the expert!
Next Steps and Recommendations for Future Research	• How you can possibly expand your study • In hindsight, what else needs to be studied in that topic area.	• Have fun and be creative.
Conclusion	• Ties it all together	• Short, sweet, and to the point.

INTERPRETATION OF FINDINGS FOR RESEARCH QUESTIONS AND HYPOTHESES AND ADDITIONAL ANALYSES: WHAT?

This is part of the study that requires that you be Creative because you have to think critically about why the data turned out that way. You have to reflect on what might have impacted the data throughout the study process. Unique characteristics that emerged from the data should be considered when you evaluate them. This section is generally organized by each research question and hypothesis, followed by additional analyses, if applicable.

To interpret the findings, take a step back from the study and try to look at it as objectively as possible to decipher the nature of the results and what they mean. Your Chair and other Committee Members will most likely want to share their input on the meaning of the data, so it is important to check in with them after you complete the data analyses.

The data are the data, but they have their defining traits. For instance, if you did a cross-sectional study on anxiety in New York City and you could only collect the data shortly after 9/11, when terrorists crashed airplanes into the World Trade Center; the Pentagon in Washington, DC; and into an open field in Pennsylvania, you would have to consider the tragic and historical events of that day when interpreting the results. Yes, these threaten validity, as mentioned in Chapter 6, but it is also a general characteristic of the study's sample at that single moment in time, like a still snapshot taken from a camera. The profound impact of those catastrophic events would be a characteristic of the data. If you collected these data only in the New York metropolitan area, you probably could not generalize the data to a population from another city that might not have had as much of a direct impact from 9/11. They might have felt the angst of the day, but not like the New Yorkers.

Sometimes the data characteristics might impact your ability to generalize or apply these data to another population. Another example of a study with data that is not easily generalizable is if you did a study on romantic relationships using a sample that was 90% 19-year-old boys and applied it to the global adult population. Obviously, 19-year-old boys and other age groups, like middle-aged women, are not likely to share the same opinion of relationships! The inability to generalize is also a limitation of the data, which is mentioned in the next section.

Limitations

As much as we try to do our best, there is no such thing as a perfect research study. Unfortunately, every study has limitations, study features that threaten the quality and validity of the data. This section requires us to humbly reflect on some of the study's flaws. We can only plan and control for what we can anticipate, but surprise issues are likely to emerge throughout the study process and are considered to be limitations. Some common limitations include:

- Sample size that is too small.
- Homogeneous (alike) sample that lacks diversity, such as a sample from mostly one gender or age group.
- Data collection tools that lack evidence of validity and reliability.
- Bad timing of data collection or study events, such as situations that could impact results from a group, organization, or community.
- Confounding variables, which are variables that surprisingly emerged during the study process, such as test anxiety during a cognitive ability test.

Even the best studies have limitations, so it's best to acknowledge them, but do not let them make you feel stuck. They are typical research study imperfections, so move on.

IMPLICATIONS FOR THEORY AND PRACTICE: SO WHAT?

Now that you have collected original data, you are officially a player and an expert in your topic. This section also requires Creativity because here you get to present and even, perhaps, show off what you know by applying your data to the world of practice and adding to the theoretical models in your field. This is where you think critically about the data and talk about what the results really mean (Cone & Foster, 2006). This is one of my favorite phases of research study because I get to think of a role for the data.

Brainstorming implications might require a great deal of soul searching. Here are some questions you could ask yourself about the data:

- How do these results challenge or support the theoretical models and empirical research cited in the Literature Review?
- What was learned from these results in layman, not scholarly, terms?
- How can these results be used to help people or systems?
- What do these data mean for your field?

Your Committee will want to discuss these with you as well. They should have some good ideas.

FUTURE RESEARCH: NOW WHAT?

You just contributed brand-spanking-new research to the field. Knowing what you know, what are some next steps for the data? What suggestions do you have for follow-up studies? Here are typical recommendations for future research:

- Replicate study with a different population.
- Replicate study with a different way to measure the same construct.
- Replicate study in a different location, context, or time frame.
- Replicate study, but modify interventions or other activities.
- New research that stems from the foundation of these current study findings.
- Reinvent current study for a new study.

CONCLUSION

A final conclusion follows the future research section. The conclusion is a few paragraphs that summarize the findings and overall dissertation. Not only are you concluding the Discussion chapter, but the entire dissertation. Make this strong because in many cases this is the only part of the dissertation that gets read by anyone other than the Committee!

CHAPTER KILLERS

Discussion Chapter Killers

You are begging Committee Members for revisions if you do any of the following:

- Use first person instead of third person.
- Claim that the study had no limitations.
- Ignore the limitations and try to inappropriately generalize the study.
- Do not connect your data to scholarly literature on theory and practice.
- Provide a view of the results that lacks your unique interpretation.

I find it easy to achieve flow (Cziksentmihalyi, 1991) when writing discussions since I feel like I have no choice but to be immersed in the data; it feels invigorating to brainstorm how to use it. Let yourself shine. After you finish the reference list (this has to be perfect, in APA format with no references missing), it's time to start preparing for the Oral Defense, which is the last official challenge of this process, meaning you are in the home stretch of finishing your dissertation and ending this ordeal! Chapter 10 talks about preparing for the Oral Defense and thinking about possible next steps for your dissertation study data, which is optional, of course.

CHAPTER TEN

Your Data's Next Chapter After the Dissertation Write-Up and Graduation

Congratulations on finishing your dissertation! You spent hours and hours researching, reading, writing, writing, writing, revising, more revising, and now you are finally done! I am sure you know this by now, but the dissertation process comes with emotional ups and downs; hopefully, completing the five chapters is filled with a great deal of joy, as well as many other emotions. But you're not finished yet. You just need to get through your Oral Defense, also known as "the Defense" so you can graduate and resume your life.

It is now time to prepare for the Defense and think about whether there is anything else you want to do with your data after it; and if so, what? You are officially an expert with fresh empirical evidence, so why not do something with it before the data get stale? I highly suggest you try to use the data to help build your career through options like presenting at a conference, publishing in a journal, and applying your data via a consulting situation.

POINTERS FOR A SMOOTH ORAL DEFENSE

The Defense is commonly the last step of the dissertation hazing process before being admitted into the Doctor's Club. It is when the committee gathers and you answer questions regarding your study, such as the research design, theoretical lens, methodology (e.g., "why was Instrument A chosen over Instrument B?"), how you analyzed the results, and your suggested implications. They can throw anything they want at you, so be prepared to explain every number and study feature.

You walk in the Oral as Ms./Mrs./Mr. _____ and walk out as Dr. _____. The Defense itself is a meeting led by an Examining Chairperson, who is likely to be a recommendation of your Chair. He or she will facilitate the questioning process and manage the discussions. The myth is that the Defense is a pass or fail process, but in most cases, it is not. Under most circumstances, when the Committee supports the decision that you set up the Defense, they are hoping to pass you. If a Committee Member raises concerns about you or your data's readiness for the Defense, you should address it with that Member. If there seems to be a real issue, be open to rescheduling the Defense until it is resolved. You want to walk out of the Defense with as few revisions as possible, which is why you "defend" your work.

It is essential that you go with the flow during the Defense. Remember, like the entire dissertation process, the Defense is not just about you. Aside from Emotional and Social Intelligence (refer to the list in Chapter 1) in managing your own emotions and feeling in tune with the Committee (Goleman, Boyatzis, & McKee, 2002), here are some additional pointers for preparing for the Defense (Cone & Foster, 2006):

- Rehearse—there is no such thing as being overprepared.
- Create visuals or handouts if necessary.
- Be ready to explain every result and how you got there.
- Dress professionally by wearing a suit or a jacket/blazer and pants (the type that are typically dry clean only) or skirt, as well as shined shoes. If you want to be a doctor, look like one.
- Ask each committee member his/her expectations of you before the Defense.
- Be able to speak proudly about every aspect of your methodology, such as why you chose your sample, instruments, and materials, as well as procedure, despite limitations.
- Be ready to explain how you would conduct the study over again, with and without limited resources.
- Suggest ideas for future research such as what you would do to take the data to the next level.
- Provide implications of how these data fit into the real world of applied practice and theoretical models.
- Humbly acknowledge the study's limitations.
- Share what you learned about yourself, the process, and the topic.
- Know why you choose each and every source in your literature review, how you feel about that source's work, and how they would interpret your work.
- Be prepared to interpret your findings through other relevant theoretical models.
- Be as calm and relaxed as possible (I highly recommend a massage the night before).
- Know and follow your department's norms about bringing visitors and food into the Defense.
- Expect side tangents, and do not interrupt them. Remember, it's not entirely about you—meaning in the middle of responding to a question, you might get cut off by

a Committee Member, which could lead to a side conversation or debate that does not include you. Just go with it.
- You will know when it is over. You might be asked to leave the room so the Committee can discuss and decide on your revisions.

After the Defense, you will integrate the Committee's suggestions for improvement, to their exact specifications, and hand in what will be your final draft. Your Chair might give it one more read before it is officially approved. Bear in mind that additional revisions are not unusual. Continue to be humble and make the changes. The Committee is committed to make your dissertation the best it can be, even if it means more work for you. I highly recommend that you make the changes suggested by the Committee right away while still fresh. After you get the Committee's signatures, hand them in and wait to hear when you are receiving your diploma, Doctor! Don't forget to bind the final copy of your dissertation to keep on your favorite bookshelf.

REALITY CHECK

I vividly remember feeling very shocked when my Defense was all over. Shortly after I was kicked out of the room, Frank opened the door and yelled, "Congratulations, Dr. Broder!" I am not sure what was more surreal—knowing I was finally done or being called Dr. Broder. The shock eventually wore off, but it definitely took months.

POSTGRADUATION WORDS OF WISDOM

The prominent and legendary Dr. Philip G. Zimbardo, Professor Emeritus of Psychology at Stanford University, current core faculty at Palo Alto University, and past president of the American Psychological Association, said it best in an inspiring graduation speech that he delivered to newly minted Psychology graduates. Dr. Zimbardo is a dynamic first-generation scholar, so you can only imagine the energy when he delivered his motivating graduation speech, which he ended with his Ten Paths for Your Perfect Life—After Graduation.

Ten Paths for Your Perfect Life—After Graduation

1. Never stop being a student—be filled with curiosity and wonder, ask why, discover how.
2. Make time for family, friends, and fun—especially when you are really busy doing "stuff."
3. Let compassion be your guiding light, but heroic action your daily goal.
4. Trade in familiar habits for novel adventures.
5. Nurture your passions; tolerate all the rest.
6. Violate expectations to liberate yourself from predictability.
7. Take risks, learn from mistakes, try harder, and think wiser next time around.
8. Develop a balanced time perspective—well grounded in the past, linking to your family and culture, be energized by the power of the present and motivated to succeed by a hope-filled future.
9. Be the engaging host at life's party, not its reluctantly shy guest.
10. Change the world for the better—people, situations, and systems—each day in some way, by what you stand for, and the wrongs you are willing to challenge with righteous integrity.

Excerpted from Dr. Philip G. Zimbardo's (Professor Emeritus of Psychology, Stanford University, and former president of APA) speech at the Stanford University Psychology Department in June 2012.

Graduating and accomplishing such a big goal brings an assortment of different emotions for everyone. Thankfully, pride and joy are among them, but any emotion you feel is acceptable. Staying connected with other graduates, both recent and past, is helpful so you can support and mentor each other through whatever you are feeling. For me, it was pure shock and I am not sure why. I know other people who felt a sense of let down. It was what it was.

YOUR DISSERTATION BEYOND GRADUATION (IF AND WHEN YOU ARE READY, OF COURSE)

After you graduate, celebrate, and regroup, what is next? After you decompress from the dissertation process, ideally you are still Passionate about your topic enough to do something with your data. If not, no problem, just come back to this if and when you are ready.

Preferably, you conducted a Rigorous and Creative study that shed a great deal of insight into your particular topic and want to share it among the community of content experts. Since you are officially in the Doctor's Club, you are one of them, so show off what you know. You have three main options: present at a conference, publish in a scholarly journal, or apply the data toward a consultation project or job you might want.

Present at a Conference

There are many excellent professional organizations in the social sciences and almost all of them hold annual conventions or conferences. The American Psychological Association (APA), American Educational Research Association (AERA), and Association for Psychological Science (APS) are the largest groups in education and psychology. These larger organizations have smaller chapters by content specialties. For example, in the APA, there are 56 specialized subgroups called divisions, and examples include Educational Psychology, Society for Industrial and Organization Psychologists, Clinical Psychology, and Society for Media Psychology and Technology. Thus, there are annual opportunities to present your work either via presentation or poster session. Either way, you are getting your work out there, meeting people, learning, earning continuing education credits (if you have a psychology license to maintain), and networking.

If you are looking for a place to start, I recommend joining one of the bigger organizations. I have happily been a member of the APA since I was a student. Joining and becoming active in divisions are excellent for meeting people and building your Network with other scholars and practitioners who may share the Passion for your area of expertise. During an annual convention, you can get to know their Network and, if you want, learn how you can become involved in the division and about smaller conferences or groups subdivided by state or region. In addition, there are always leadership opportunities to serve on the division executive boards.

REALITY CHECK

Like applying to the Institutional Review Board (IRB), a conference or journal submission requires following directions when completing the application and the standards and criticisms are higher now that you are a doctor. For instance, when they say "describe in one paragraph," they mean *one* paragraph. If you choose not to agree with revisions or suggestions for improvement, chances are that your conference or journal submission will automatically be rejected.

Publish Your Study in a Scholarly Journal

Another way to put your work out there is to turn your dissertation study into an article to be submitted to a peer-reviewed, scholarly journal. This means you have to trim your 150-page (or so) book into a 20-page (average, but submission requirements vary per journal) article. Most journals in the social sciences require APA format (so your *Publication Manual* is an investment). Typical article layout includes a pithy version of the:

- Introduction
- Literature review
- Research questions and hypotheses
- Research design
- Participants
- Instruments and materials
- Procedure
- Results
- Discussion

It is common that your Chair or one of the Committee members will want to collaborate with you on this so they can mentor you through the process. In terms of authorship, I think that the student should be the first author and faculty should be the subsequent authors. However, it might not be your decision if you want to collaborate so just roll with the punches.

Receiving an "Accept As Is" letter can be a long process that can take up to a year, depending on the number of resubmissions. As a journal editor, my observation is that most manuscripts need at least a round or two (maybe three or four) of revisions before they are accepted. I think only once did I see a paper earn an "Accept As Is" on the first go-around, but it was an excellent paper written by three authors who had many years each of publishing and editing experience.

The manuscript rejection rate is high, so do not be discouraged if your paper gets rejected, with no option to revise and resubmit. Whether your paper gets accepted or not, you should (but not always will) get detailed feedback from the reviewers. However, some of the types of feedback will vary per reviewer; some will provide a great deal of detail and others do not. Journal reviewers are typically prominent content experts who were hand chosen by the editors: meaning, they know their stuff. Even if your paper gets outright rejected, you will probably get feedback so you can possibly resubmit to another journal. There are hundreds of journals to send your work to, so keep trying. The journals out there vary in terms of the type of Rigor they look for in a study, but if your study has real-world implications, you are bound to have some journal accept your work at some point. Learn from the criticism, don't take it personally or as an insult and try not to be disheartened by it, even if it is painful. You will only learn from your mistakes!

Apply Your Study Data as Consultation Content

When we feel Passionate about a topic, we want to see how it works in the real world. If you know of a group, system, or organization that might benefit from your data, I encourage you to reach out to them. Perhaps your data can be used to create an intervention or consultation project for a client. For instance, for a study on online shopping behavior, learning what makes people want to shop on the Internet, the data could be used to create a workshop that helps people with Internet shopping addiction.

REALITY CHECK

Remember, the number one rule of consulting is that it is not about you, it's about the client. Even if it is about your study data, you are using it to improve a group, system, or organization; the client's needs come first.

Consulting is an art and a science (Tilin, 2011), and I highly suggest that you have a basic understanding about the process. At the end of this chapter, there is a list that suggests additional references to help you learn how to consult. Figure 10.1 shows a life cycle for a consulting process developed over the past 20 years by Felice Tilin, PhD, who has worked as a coach and consultant to multinational companies and organizations.

In the case of offering your dissertation data to help, you have that data, but you need to work with the client on how it might benefit them. A good consultant is authentic and client-centered. Of course, it should be a win/win situation (Covey, 1989) with mutual benefits for you and the potential client. I strongly suggest that you put together a project proposal, which Tilin (2011) refers to as contracting, so everybody is

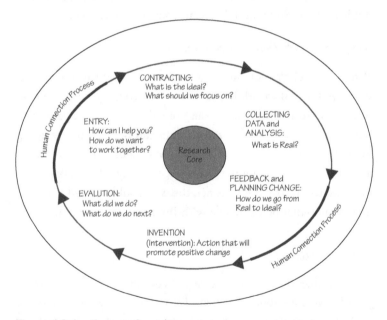

Figure 10.1 Process Consulting
© 2011 Felice J. Tilin, GroupWorks Consulting, www.groupworksglobal.com

clear about roles and expectations. Project proposals should include:

- Project purpose
- Project goals
- Project activities to fulfill those goals
- Deliverables
- Your role
- Client's role
- Timeline
- Budget (if necessary)

Through your consultation project, you will learn about your data on a different level. You might also think of suggestions for future research that you could use to mentor someone else through their process. As an expert, you can give back to the community of research and practice.

In addition to consulting, you can also use you data to bring you closer to employment opportunities. You can use these data to help leverage job opportunities. The world is yours, Doctor!

Closing Thoughts

I hope you had a fabulous celebration, because you certainly earned it. Goal accomplishment should not be taken for granted, especially finishing such a big project as a dissertation. I also hope that the dissertation was an intellectually stimulating project that will enhance your career. However, most important, you finished it! May this experience be a motivator, as well as help you to accomplish more and be someone else's Interpersonal Strength for their dissertation process.

Thank you for reading this book, and all the best in your future career. Please do not hesitate to contact me at joannebrodersumerson@gmail.com if you want to share any valuable feedback with me.

Appendix A
Summary Chart of Statistics, What to Report, Abbreviations, and Suggested Syntax

Statistic	What to Report	Abbreviation	Suggested Syntax
Frequencies and Percentages	Size of overall data set	N	Respondents were recruited from communication courses (N = 65).
	Size of a cell or group	n	Males represented a smaller proportion of the sample (n = 25) than women (n = 40).
	Percentages	%	Of those participating in the study, only 35% were aware of the manipulation
Mean and Standard Deviation	Mean	M	The mean of group one (M = 3.25, SD = 1.12) was greater than the mean of group two (M = 2.45, SD = 0.99).
	Dispersion measure	SD	
Cronbach's Alpha	Observed reliability coefficient	α (Cronbach's alpha)	α = .80 Cronbach's alpha = .80
	Descriptive statistics	M and SD	

Cohen's Kappa and Scott's Pi	Observed reliability coefficient	κ (Cohen's kappa)/ π (Scott's pi)	$\kappa = .80$ Cohen's kappa = .80 $\pi = .80$ Scott's Pi = .80
	Percentage of agreement		
	Number of items coded to establish reliability		
	Number of coders		
Spearman Rank-Order Correlation	Degrees of freedom	df	$r_s(df) = observed\ r_s\ value,$ significance level
	Observed r_s value	r_s	
	Significance level	p	
Pearson Product-Moment Correlation	Observed r value	r	$r(df) = observed\ r\ value,$ significance level
	Significance level	p	
	Degrees of freedom	df	
	Descriptive statistics	M and SD	

(Continued)

129

Statistic	What to Report	Abbreviation	Suggested Syntax
Chi-Square Tests	Degrees of freedom	df	$\chi^2(df, N = XX) =$ observed chi-square value, significance level, ES
	Number of observations	N	
	Observed chi-square value	χ^2	
	Significance level	p	
	Effect size	ES (varies with test)	
	Number of observations per cell	n	
	Table of frequencies/ percentages	(optional)	
Wilcoxon Rank Sum Test/Mann-Whitney U Test	Observed z or U value	z/U	Group 1 (n = XX) was greater than Group 2 (n = XX), z[or U] = observed z[or U] value, significance level, ES
	Significance level	p	
	Effect size	ES (varies with test)	
	Number of observations	N	
	Number of observations per group	n	
	Mean ranks		
Kruskal-Wallis Test	Degrees of freedom	df	$H(df, N = XX) =$ observed H value, significance level, ES

130

Number of observations	N	
Observed test value	H (or χ^2)	
Significance level	p	
Effect size	ES (varies with test)	
Number of observations per group	n	
Mean ranks		
McNemar's Repeated Measures Chi-Square Test for Change		
Degrees of freedom	df	$\chi^2(df, N = XX) =$ observed chi-square value, significance level, ES
Number of observations	N	
Observed chi-square value	χ^2	
Significance level	p	
Effect size	ES (varies with test)	
Number of observations per cell	n	

(Continued)

Statistic	What to Report	Abbreviation	Suggested Syntax
Cochran's Q	Degrees of freedom	*df*	$Q(df, N = XX) =$ observed test
	Number of observations	*N*	value, significance level, ES
	Value of test statistic	Q (or χ^2)	
	Significance level	*p*	
	Effect size	ES (varies with test)	
	Number of observations per cell	*n*	
Wilcoxon Signed-Rank Test	Observed test value	T (or *z*)	$N = XX$, $T =$ observed test
	Number of observations	*N*	value, significance level, ES
	Significance level	*p*	
	Effect size	ES (varies with test)	
	Rank sums (the number of +/s)	*SS*	
Friedman Analysis of Variance by Ranks Test	Descriptive statistics	*M* and *SD*	$\chi_r^2(df, N = XX) =$ observed
	Degrees of freedom	*df*	test value, significance level,
	Number of observations	*N*	ES
	Observed χ_r^2 value	χ_r^2 (or χ^2)	

	Significance level	p	
	Effect size	ES (varies with test)	
	Mean ranks		
	Number of observations per cell	n	
z Test	Degrees of freedom	df	z(df) = observed z value, sig-
	Observed z value	z	nificance level, ES
	Significance level	p	
	Effect size	ES (varies with test)	
	Number of observations	N	
	Sample mean and standard deviation	M and SD	

(Continued)

Statistic	What to Report	Abbreviation	Suggested Syntax
t Test	Degrees of freedom	df	$t(df)$ = observed t value, significance level, ES
	Observed t value	t	
	Significance level	p	
	Effect size	ES (varies with test)	
	Number of observations	N	
	Number of observations per cell	n	
	Descriptive statistics	M and SD	
Analysis of Variance (ANOVA)	Degrees of freedom (between and within)	df_B/df_W	$F(df_B/df_W)$ = observed F value, significance level, ES
	Observed F value	F	
	Significance level	p	
	Effect size	ES (varies with test)	
	Number of observations	N	
	Number of observations per cell	n	
	Descriptive statistics	M and SD	

ANCOVA	What to report (in addition to ANOVA)	
	Adjusted means	adj M
	Covariate information (regression format)	

For main effects and interactions: $F(df_B / df_W) = $ observed F value, significance level, ES (accompanied by a table of adjusted group and cell means and standard deviations)

For covariate analyses: $F(df_B / df_W) = $ observed F value, significance level, partial ES (after covariates are removed). Accompanying table of pooled within-cell intercorrelations among the covariates and the dependent variable

(Continued)

Statistic	What to Report	Abbreviation	Suggested Syntax
MANOVA	Multivariate statistic	(varies) Wilks lambda, Pillais	Wilks lambda = observed λ value, $F(df_B, df_W)$ = observed F value, significance level, ES
	Degrees of freedom (between and within)	df_B / df_W	
	Observed F value	F	
	Significance level	p	
	Effect size	ES (varies with test)	
	Univariate effects	(see ANOVA)	
	Number of observations	N	
	Number of observations per cell	n	
	Descriptive statistics	M and SD	
MANCOVA	What to report (in addition to MANOVA)		See ANCOVA
	Adjusted means	adj M	
	Covariate information (regression format)		

136

Regression and Multiple Regression	Overall Model		
	Multiple R	R	For the model: $F(df_B, df_W) =$ observed F value, significance level, R^2, adj R^2 (accompanied by table with unstandardized regression coefficient, standardized regression coefficients)
	Effect size	R^2	
	Adjusted R^2	adj R^2	
	Observed F	F	
	Degrees of freedom	df	
	Significance level	p	
	Predictors		Individual relationships between the independent variables and dependent variables: $t =$ observed t value, significance level, effect size
	Unstandardized regression coefficient	B	
	Standardized regression coefficient	β	
	Observed t value	t	
	Significance level	p	
	Semipartial correlations	(variance accounted for per variable)	

(Continued)

Statistic	What to Report	Abbreviation	Suggested Syntax
Logistic Regression	*Overall Model*		R^2 = observed R^2 value, χ^2(df,
	Observed χ^2 value	χ^2	N = number of observations
	Effect size	R^2	= observed χ^2 value, signifi-
	Degrees of freedom	df	cance level
	Number of observations	N	
	Significance level	p	
	Classification results	(optional)	
	Predictors		
	Standardized regression coefficient	β	
	Observed Wald χ^2 value	χ^2	
	Significance level	p	
	Odds ratio		

From Numbers to Words: Reporting Statistical Results for the Social Sciences by S. E. Morgan, T. Reichert, and T. R. Harrison, 2002, Upper Saddle River, NJ: Pearson Education. Copyright 2002. Reprinted by permission of Pearson Education, Inc.

Appendix B

Anatomy of a Dissertation in Context

(Insert Your Title)

In Partial Fulfillment for the Degree Requirement_____

Your Name
University

Abstract

The Abstract should be a pithy summary of the study that includes the problem, research questions, brief description of method, general conclusions, and implications. For the proposal, the Abstract should be written in future tense; use past tense with a quick summary of the results for the final write-up.

Points to remember:

- This is often the future reader's first exposure to your study.
- The Abstract sells the research; it needs to be a quick advertisement with all of the information listed above, so that picky consumers of research will know whether or not to read about your study.
- The same Abstract guidelines apply to dissertations and journal articles.
- This needs to be strong and clear.

TABLE OF CONTENTS

The Table of Contents tells the reader where to find each chapter, subchapter, table, figure, and appendix.

Good news: Microsoft Word has a feature that will format this.

DEDICATION

A dedication is not necessary, but it is a very nice thing to do. It is a tre-mendous honor to a person or people who show you unconditional support.

Appendix B

ACKNOWLEDGMENTS

The Acknowledgment section gives you the opportunity to thank the Committee, Interpersonal Strength, and Network for their friendship, love, encouragement, support, and guidance. I personally think it is tacky when people do not have an Acknowledgment. Never forget where you came from or the people who supported you while you achieved success.

The format for Acknowledgments sections will vary because they are so personal. Do not forget anybody!

Chapter One (Introduction)

Introduction to the Introduction

This chapter subsection includes:

- Cited literature to set the stage for your study.
- Trends, issues, and background of this topic.

Points to remember:

- Grab reader's attention with first sentence.

Rationale

This chapter subsection includes:

- Statements regarding importance of topic.
- Detailed explanation of the problem.
- Mention of gaps in the literature or lack of knowledge in practice.

Points to remember:

- Continue to convince the reader why a study on this topic was needed.

Purpose of Study

This chapter subsection includes:

- A clear statement that stems from *"the purpose of this study was to . . ."*
- Expansion of this to talk about how your data could be applied to improve a situation.

Points to remember:

- Purpose statement should be strong, crisp, and pithy.
- Include a brief description of methodology.
- Discuss the relevance of data and how it will be used to improve this and that.

CHAPTER TWO (LITERATURE REVIEW)

This chapter generally includes:

- Synthesis of published, peer reviewed, and scholarly works of theory, models, empirical data, and case studies for each variable.
- The frame of your perspective.
- Historical trends, themes, and gaps.

Points to remember:

- This chapter is typically organized by variable; many, many drafts will help you determine the right sequence for your study.
- If you were not the very first one to say, research, or notice it, then it must be cited.
- More is always better when it comes to empirical evidence from previous research studies.
- Use citations over quotations.
- Use direct quotes *only* to make a strong statement.

Conceptual Definitions

This chapter subsection includes:

- Description of each dependent and independent variable, as explained in the literature.

Points to remember:

- This chapter is different than the operational definition that belongs in the Methodology chapter.

Chapter Three (Methodology)

Research Questions and Hypotheses

This chapter subsection includes:

- One hypothesis per research question.

Points to remember:

- The research questions are the foundation for the entire study.
- They should echo each other.
- Format so that they look like this:
  RQ 1:
  HY 1:
  RQ 2:
  HY 2:

Research Design

This chapter subsection includes:

- Description of research design and how it was chosen for the study.
- How the data will be analyzed.

Points to remember:

- The type of study, number of groups involved.
- This is more big-picture information, as opposed to detail.

Operational Definitions

This chapter subsection includes:

- Brief definition of independent and dependent variables.

Points to remember:

- This definition is concrete and measurable (e.g., how much, how often, scores between x and y).
- Differs from the conceptual definition in the Literature Review, in that it is not theoretical.

Participants

This chapter subsection includes:

- Description of participants.
- What made them eligible for the study.
- How they were recruited for your study.
- Description of any compensation.

Points to remember:

- Provide a very clear picture of study sample.
- Mention how you maintained their privacy.

Instruments and Materials

This chapter subsection includes:

- Detailed description of any surveys, activities, programs, and other materials used for your study.
- Rationale for using those materials.
- For published instruments, include a summary of validation process and other psychometric properties to support robustness.
- For homemade surveys, talk about the validation process to support that they will basically be "good enough" or the only option for your study.

Points to remember:

- Provide a clear visual for the reader about the looks of your materials and their length of administration.
- Surveys and other study materials belong in the appendixes.
- Be confident in your explanation as to why the instrument and materials were used.

Procedure

This chapter subsection includes:

- Detailed description of what you did when you collected the data.
- Tell the reader the full story from start to finish.

Points to remember:

- The more detail, the better, so that anyone could replicate your procedure to the letter.

Chapter Four (Results)

Introduction

This chapter subsection includes:

- Summary of the purpose of the study and methodology.
- Description of the process or application for data analysis.

Points to remember:

- Keep it short, sweet, and to the point.
- Just say what you did to analyze the data.

Descriptive Data

This chapter subsection includes:

- Frequency analyses of number and percentage of relevant demographic groups (e.g., gender, age group, nationality, etc.).

Points to remember:

- You do not have to include any SPSS codes.
- You may need to include a table for this.

Analyses of Research Questions and Hypotheses

This chapter subsection includes:

- Presented by each research question and hypothesis with a summary, table, or figure of the data that either supports or challenges the hypothesis.
- Brief mention of whether it supports or challenges the literature.

Points to remember:

- Write statistics in proper format (see statistical chart in Appendix A).
- Eliminate bias; the data should be unfolded and connected very objectively.
- Tell it like it is.
- Don't skimp on the real evidence.

Additional Analyses

This chapter subsection includes:

- Other observations or patterns in your data that you find worth mentioning.
- Brief mention on how it fits into the literature.

Points to remember:

- Write statistics in proper format (see statistical chart in Appendix A).
- Eliminate bias; the data should be unfolded and connected very objectively.
- Tell it like it is.
- Don't skimp on the real evidence.

CHAPTER FIVE (DISCUSSION)

Introduction

This chapter subsection includes:

- Very brief summary of the purpose of the study, method, and how the data were analyzed.

Points to remember:

- Keep it short, sweet, and to the point.

Interpretation of the Findings

This chapter subsection includes:

- Organization per research question or additional analyses.
- Discussion of the results, their meaning, their connection to the literature, and how the data could be used.

Points to remember:

- Be creative; this is one of the fun parts.
- Why do you think the data turned out that way?

Limitations

This chapter subsection includes:

- Any feature about the study that might hinder the data from being generalized.

Points to remember:

- Swallow your pride and be humble.

Implications for Theory and Practice

This chapter subsection includes:

- Your interpretation of the overall meaning of the data, as well as how it fits into the literature and "real world."

Points to remember:

- Be assertive; you are now an expert in this topic.
- Think of this as settling the argument in the literature.

Next Steps and Recommendations for Future Research

This chapter subsection includes:

- A discussion of how you can possibly expand your study.
- Knowing what you know now, what else needs to be studied in that topic area?

Points to remember:

- Have fun and be creative.

Conclusion

This chapter subsection includes:

- A few paragraphs to wrap up the chapter and entire study.

Points to remember:

- Ties it all together.
- Keep it short, sweet, and to the point.

REFERENCES

This section includes:

- Formatted APA style (see *Publication Manual of the American Psychological Association*; APA, 2010).
- Every single reference needs to be listed in this section.

Appendixes

Included in this section:

- Documents that might be too big to place in the body of the text, including, but not limited to, instruments, participant recruitment protocols, raw data, tables, figures, and pictures.

Points to Remember:

- Each separate document in the appendixes should be named and numbered.

Appendix C
Sample Dissertation Rubric

1. **Strength of argument for study rationale was:**
   Guiding statement: The candidate did a _____ job selling the study.

0	1	2	3	4
Poor	Fair	Decent	Very Good	Exemplary

   Comments:

2. **Quality of literature review was:**
   Guiding statement: The use of citations, theory, and previous research was _____.

0	1	2	3	4
Poor	Fair	Decent	Very Good	Exemplary

Comments:

3. **Description of methodology was:**
   Guiding statement: The walk through of the data collection process was _____.

0	1	2	3	4
Poor	Fair	Decent	Very Good	Exemplary

Comments:

4. **There was a clear connection between the literature review, research questions, hypotheses, and data collection items.**
   Guiding Statement: The variables were linked well throughout the study.

0	1	2	3
Strongly Disagree	Disagree	Agree	Strongly Agree

Comments:

5. **Results aligned with the research questions and hypotheses**.

    Guiding statement: The data answered the research question very well.

0	1	2	3
Strongly Disagree	Disagree	Agree	Strongly Agree

Comments:

6. **Description of results was:**

    Guiding statement: The results were presented with appropriate use of tables.

0	1	2	3	4
Poor	Fair	Decent	Very Good	Exemplary

Comments:

7. **Discussion was:**

    Guiding statement: The discussion was well presented, including limitations and future research?

0	1	2	3	4
Poor	Fair	Decent	Very Good	Exemplary

Comments:

8. **Implications highlighted connections between research, literature, and real world.**

   Guiding statement: The candidate seemed to understand and apply the study results.

0	1	2	3
Strongly Disagree	Disagree	Agree	Strongly Agree

   Comments:

9. **Dissertation mostly followed the manuscript guidelines of APA style.**

   Guiding statement: The candidate mostly followed the Publication Manual, 6th edition?

0	1	2	3
Strongly Disagree	Disagree	Agree	Strongly Agree

Comments:

10. **Dissertation was structured according to the Anatomy of a Dissertation.**

    Guiding statement: The candidate followed the directions and guidelines of the Anatomy of a Dissertation.

0	1	2	3
Strongly Disagree	Disagree	Agree	Strongly Agree

Comments:

11. **Overall quality of dissertation was:**

0	1	2	3	4
Poor	Fair	Decent	Very Good	Exemplary

Comments:

Overall point total:___/35
General feedback:

Appendix D
The Juicers

EMPIRICAL JUICER

Full reference:

Purpose of study:

Argument/Logic developed in the literature review:

Research questions:

Hypothesis:

Research design:

Participants:

Independent variables:

Dependent variables:

Instrumentation/Materials:

Procedure:

How did they analyze their data?

General conclusions:

Implications:

Study strengths:

Limitations:

Confounding variables:

What does this study add to my lit review?

Which chapters does this article fit?

Which other sources connect with this study?

Miscellaneous notes:

THEORETICAL JUICER

Full reference:

Fundamental principles:

Strengths:

Limitations:

Recommendations:

What does this study add to my lit review?

Which chapters does this article fit?

Which other sources connect with this study?

Miscellaneous notes:

References

Adair, J. (1984). The Hawthorne effect: A reconsideration of the methodological artifact. *Journal of Applied Psychology, 69*(2), 334–345.

American Psychological Association. (2010). *Publication manual of the American Psychological Association* (6th ed.). Washington, DC: Author.

Boyatzis, R. (1998). *Transforming qualitative information: Thematic analysis and code development.* Thousand Oaks, CA: Sage.

Campbell, D., & Stanley, J. (1963). *Experimental and quasi-experimental designs for research.* Boston, MA: Houghton Mifflin.

Cohen, J. (1982). A power primer. *Psychological Bulletin, 112*(1), 155–159.

Cone, J., & Foster, S. (2006). *Dissertations and theses from start to finish: Psychology and related fields* (2nd ed.). Washington, DC: American Psychological Association.

Costa, P. T., & McRae, R. R. (1995). Domains and factors: Hierarchical personality assessment using the Revised NEO Personality Inventory. *Journal of Personality Assessment, 64,* 21–50.

Covey, S. (1989). *The 7 habits of highly effective people: Powerful lessons in personal change.* New York, NY: Fireside.

Creswell, J. (2009). *Research design: Qualitative, quantitative, and mixed methods approaches* (3rd ed.). Thousand Oaks, CA: Sage.

Csikszentmihalyi, M. (1991). *Flow: The psychology of optimal experience.* New York, NY: Harper Perennial.

Davis, G., & Parker, C. (1997). *Writing the doctoral dissertation: A systemic approach* (2nd ed.). Hauppauge, NY: Barron's Educational Series.

Eissenberg, T., Paniker, S., Berenbaum, S., Epley, N., Fendrich, M., Kelso, R., . . . Simmerling, M. (2004). *IRBs and psychological science: Ensuring a collaborative relationship.* Retrieved from http://www.apa.org/research/responsible/irbs-psych-science.pdf

Fowler, F. (1995). *Improving survey questions: Design and evaluation.* Thousand Oaks, CA: Sage.

Glass, G. (1976). Primary, secondary, and meta-analysis of research. *Educational Researcher, 5*(10), 3–8.

Glenn, D. (2010, March 31). Help to the finish line: Ways to reduce the number of Ph.D. dropouts. *Chronicle of Higher Education.* Retrieved from http://chronicle.com/article/Help-to-the-Finish-Line-Ways/64879/

Goleman, D., Boyatzis, R., & McKee, A. (2002). *Primal leadership: Learning to lead with emotional intelligence.* Boston, MA: Harvard Business School Press.

Kaufman, J. (2009). *Creativity 101.* New York, NY: Springer.

Kaufman, J., & Beghetto, R. (2009). Beyond big and little: The Four C Model of Creativity. *Review of General Psychology, 13*(1), 1–12.

Messick, S. (1995). Validity of psychological assessment: Validation of inferences from person's responses and performances as scientific inquiry into score meaning. *American Psychologist, 50*(9), 741–749.

Morgan, S.E., Reichert, T., & Harrison, T.R. (2002). *From numbers to words: reporting statistical results for the social sciences.* Upper Saddle River, NJ: Pearson Education.

Park, J. H. (2013). Keynote speech delivered at the International Group Development Questionnaire Conference at Saint Joseph's University, Philadelphia, PA.

Payne, S. (1951). *The art of asking questions.* Princeton, NJ: Princeton University Press.

Philippe, F., Vallerand, R., Halfort, N., Lavigne, G., & Donahue, E. (2010). Passion for an activity and quality of personal relationships: The mediating role of emotions. *Journal of Personality and Social Psychology, 98*(6), 917–932.

Pryrczak, F., & Bruce, R. B. (2000). *Writing empirical research reports* (3rd ed.). Los Angeles, CA: Pryrczak Publishing.

Reynolds, C. (2010). Measurement and assessment: An editorial view. *Psychological Assessment, 22*(1), 1–4.

Salovey, P., & Mayer, J. D. (1990). Emotional intelligence. *Imagination, Cognition, and Personality, 9*(3), 185–211.

Schnee, E. (2008). "In the real world, no one drops their standards for you": Academic rigor in a college worker education program. *Equality and Excellence in Education, 41*(1), 62–80.

Silberman, M. (1998). *Active training: A handbook of techniques, designs, case examples, and tips.* San Francisco, CA: Josey-Bass/Pfeiffer.

Silvia, P. (2010). *How to write a lot: A practical guide to productive academic writing.* Washington, DC: American Psychological Association.

Spies, R. A., Carlson, J. F., & Geisinger, K. F. (Eds.), *The eighteenth mental measurements yearbook.* Lincoln: University of Nebraska Press.

Thorndike, R. L. (1982). *Applied psychometrics*. Boston, MA: Houghton Mifflin Harcourt.

Tilin, F. (2011). *Process consulting model.* Retrieved from www.groupworksglobal.com

Urdan, T. (2010). *Statistics in plain English* (3rd ed.). New York, NY: Routledge.

Wheelan, S. A., & Hochberger, J. M. (1996). Validation studies of the Group Development Questionnaire. *Small Group Research, 27*(1), 143–170.

About the Author

Dr. Joanne Broder Sumerson is a research psychologist dedicated to closing the gap between research and practice. Her research processes were developed over the years from her experiences as a seasoned research practitioner, program evaluator, consultant, professor, and, of course, former student. She has consulted to a multitude of private and public organizations. Her research and consultation interests include group process, emotional intelligence, social media, and wellness. She is a research professor and thesis advisor at Saint Joseph's University in Philadelphia, Pennsylvania. She is also the co-founding editor of *Psychology of Popular Media Culture*, published by the APA, and writes a blog, *Research Notes*, for *Psychology Today Magazine*.

In addition, she is active in the American Psychological Association. Joanne earned a PhD in Education Psychology and MEd in Adult and Organization Development from Temple University, as well as a BA in Psychology from Monmouth University. Joanne's past work experience includes prison counselor, corporate human resources generalist, and research and evaluation specialist.

Author Index

Subject Index

Subject Index